CIVIL WAR
SITES IN
GEORGIA

Other Books by Jim Miles

PATHS TO VICTORY
*A History and Tour Guide of Stones River, Chickamauga,
Chattanooga, Knoxville, and Nashville Campaigns*

PIERCING THE HEARTLAND
*A History and Tour Guide of the Fort Donelson, Shiloh, and
Perryville Campaigns*

A RIVER UNVEXED
*A History and Tour Guide of the Campaign for the
Mississippi River*

FIELDS OF GLORY
A History and Tour Guide of the Atlanta Campaign

TO THE SEA
A History and Tour Guide of Sherman's March

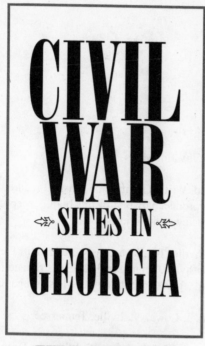

CIVIL WAR
SITES IN
GEORGIA

JIM MILES

RUTLEDGE HILL PRESS
Nashville, Tennessee

Published in Nashville, Tennessee, by Rutledge Hill Press, 211 Seventh Avenue North, Nashville, Tennessee 37219. Distributed in Canada by H. B. Fenn and Co., Ltd., 1090 Lorimar Drive, Mississauga, Ontario L5S 1R7.

Typography by E. T. Lowe, Nashville, Tennessee.

Library of Congress Cataloging-in-Publication Data

Miles, Jim.
    Civil War sites in Georgia / Jim Miles.
       p. cm.
    Includes index
    ISBN 1-55853-405-9
      1. Historic sites—Georgia—Guidebooks. 2. Georgia—Guidebooks. 3. Georgia—History—Civil War, 1861–1865. I. Title.
F287.M55 1996
917.5804'43—dc20
                               96-4597
                                  CIP

Printed in the United States of America.

1 2 3 4 5 6 7 8 9—99 98 97 96

This book is dedicated with affection and
respect to my parents,
Rayford J. and Eddie Lee Miles,
who have always encouraged my interest in
history and writing.

❧ **Contents** ❧

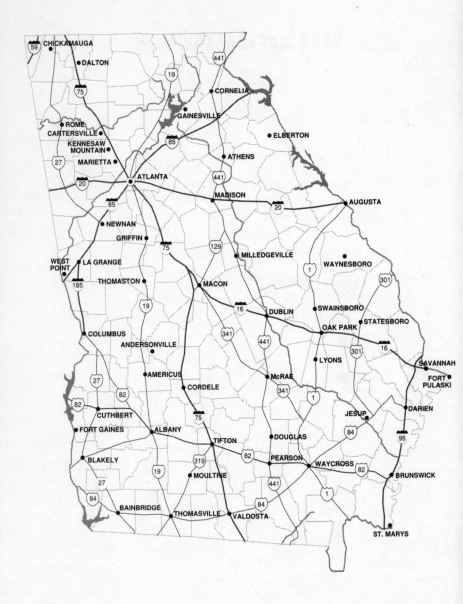

❦ **Introduction** ❦

GEORGIA WAS SO DEVASTATED during the Civil War that nearly a century was required to recover from its effects. William T. Sherman's Atlanta campaign ravaged north Georgia and concluded with the almost total destruction of the city. The legacy, however, continued with a path of devastation sixty miles wide and three hundred miles long as the invaders marched to the sea.

From the beginning of the war to its conclusion, there were 458 recorded battles and skirmishes in the state. Georgia produced 78 Confederate generals, the vice president, the secretary of state, the assistant secretaries of state, treasury, and war, and the quartermaster and commissionaire generals. Of 125,000 Georgians who served the Confederacy, 25,000 died fighting the war and more were crippled. At war's end Georgia's economy was in ruins, having lost 75 percent of its wealth, and its social and political life were nonexistent.

The state recovered. The people grieved and buried their dead. Generals and privates alike returned on foot from the disbanded armies in Virginia and North Carolina, hungry journeys that made them stronger, more determined. They planted crops and rebuilt their farms and cities. They forged a Georgia that has since become a leader of the nation, but they have never forgotten their heritage.

Georgians traditionally have taken great pride in the heroic acts and selfless sacrifices that marked their ancestors' role in the Civil War. This book is a list of the sites of significant events in Civil War Georgia and of the memorials that a battered yet defiant people raised from the ashes of defeat. These places need to be remembered, need to be visited, so we and our children can understand the epic events that have forged our character.

In touring the state and visiting these sites, please respect the rights of private home and property owners and, when required, view nonpublic sites from the street. Most communities sponsor tours of historic houses around Christmas and in the spring, providing remarkable opportunities to inspect antebellum elegance.

While a community may not have a specific Confederate cemetery, most cemeteries in Georgia have graves of Confederate veterans. Many are marked by regulation government headstones and iron crosses of honor, the latter being placed by the United Daughters of the Confederacy (UDC).

State parks and historic sites are open from 9 A.M. to 5 P.M. except Mondays. National parks operate from 8 A.M. to 5 P.M. daily. Museums and other sites maintained by municipalities and private organizations usually have limited hours and may charge admission fees. It is always wise to call ahead to determine these factors before planning a trip.

Most chapters begin with the northwesternmost county in that region and follow the first tier of counties south to the bottom of the region, then return to the top and follow the second tier of counties. Chapter 1 begins with Chickamauga and then travels south. Chapter 2 follows the Atlanta campaign through the city, and chapter 3 examines sites in metropolitan Atlanta to the west and east. Chapter 7 explores downtown Savannah, continues to Fort Pulaski, and then details sites to the north and west of the city.

Although every effort has been made to make this an exhaustive reference, the author acknowledges the possibility of having omitted sites. Information regarding museums, monuments, cemeteries, or battlefields that have been left out inadvertently may be addressed to him, care of the publisher, so that future editions can be made comprehensive.

Armies and tourists follow the same route.

■ ■

Joseph E. Brown
Mountain Campaigns in Georgia (1887)

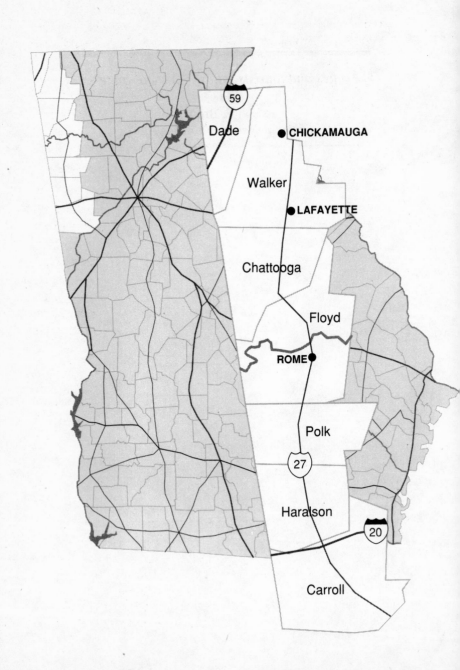

❧ 1 ❧

Chickamauga and Northwest Georgia

THE FULL FURY of the Civil War spilled into Georgia in September 1863, when Federal Gen. William S. Rosecrans drove Confederate Gen. Braxton Bragg from Middle Tennessee to Chattanooga and then forced the Confederates to evacuate that vital railroad center by flanking the town to the west through Bridgeport, Alabama. Bragg retreated into northwest Georgia to protect his railroad supply line and the industrial center of Atlanta.

Bragg was not known for his boldness, but as the direness of his situation drew the attention of Richmond and support from the Army of Northern Virginia, the Southern commander attempted to turn the tables on Rosecrans by launching a counterattack. He convinced Rosecrans that the Army of Tennessee was in full retreat, leading the Union general to divide his army unwisely and pursue the Southerners rapidly through three narrow mountain passes. Bragg ordered attacks on the isolated enemy columns, but field communications and the discipline of his subordinates broke down, and the opportunity for a decisive victory was wasted.

Rosecrans recognized the danger and concentrated his army along Chickamauga Creek on September 17. Bragg, still determined to attack, formulated a new plan to isolate Rosecrans from Chattanooga and to destroy the Union army.

Late on September 18 the first combat erupted at Reed's Bridge when Southern cavalry under the legendary Nathan Bedford Forrest drove off advancing Federal units and seized a Chickamauga Creek crossing for Bragg.

The armies finally collided on September 19. Throughout the day the conflict grew into a general battle as additional troops were added to the fight. Ultimately, sixty-six thousand Confederates confronted fifty-eight thousand Federal soldiers, one of the few times in which a Southern force outnumbered a Northern army. Confederate Gen. John B. Hood's division drove back four Union brigades at Viniard's Field, but the Federals received reinforcements and launched a counterattack that regained the position. Despite staggering casualties, Confederate and Union lines remained intact at dusk.

During the night Rosecrans's men erected crude breastworks on the wilderness battlefield, and Bragg reorganized his troops for an assault at daybreak. Gen. Leonidas Polk led the first Confederate attack, but his force was repulsed.

At midday Rosecrans was advised that a gap had formed at the center of his line, and he ordered a division from his right flank to fill the opening. But there had been no gap—the soldiers occupying the position were hidden in dense underbrush. The shifting of troops, however, created a gap on the right side of the Union line. At just that moment, Confederate Gen. James Longstreet, who had arrived the previous evening from Virginia, launched a furious attack with three divisions at the quarter-mile-wide opening. His men shattered the Union line, sending most of the Army of the Cumberland running blindly for Chattanooga through McFarlan Gap and carrying Rosecrans and two of his three corps commanders in the rout. Most of the Federals dropped their weapons and abandoned their cannon in the panic. Only one Federal corps remained on the field to continue the battle, and that unit was commanded by Gen. George W. Thomas.

Two things saved the Union army from annihilation. Col. John T. Wilder's Lightning Brigade—mounted infantry equipped with Spencer repeating rifles—staggered the advancing Confederates at the Widow Glenn's house, site of Rosecrans's headquarters the previous day. This temporarily delayed the Southern onslaught, giving Thomas time to organize the remnants of his corps on Snodgrass Hill. Longstreet soon arrived on the scene and launched three determined attacks on Thomas's strong position. When it seemed as if Thomas would be overrun, Union Gen. Gordon Granger arrived, lacking authorization to do so, with his reserve corps from Rossville in time to beat off the savage Confederate assaults mere yards from the Federal line. When darkness enveloped the field, Thomas slipped away.

On September 20 Rosecrans and his disorganized army limped into Chattanooga, expecting an immediate attack by the Southerners. Although the Confederates had won a great victory, they were too exhausted by the murderous battle to follow up on the opportunity to destroy Rosecrans. The staggering toll of casualties—thirty-four thousand—made Chickamauga the second most costly battle of the Civil War.

Chickamauga National Military Park

Chickamauga, America's first battlefield park, is the largest with five thousand acres in Georgia and three thousand in Tennessee, consisting of forests, meadows, and mountains. It is also the most frequently visited park. The park was established by Congress in 1899 at the instigation of both Federal and Confederate veterans, who raised funds with a giant barbecue at Crawfish Springs where fifteen thousand pounds of meat and thirteen thousand loaves of bread were consumed. More than ten thousand veterans of the Army of the Cumberland attended.

An estimated 1,400 historical markers in Georgia and Tennessee describe Civil War actions at Chickamauga and Chattanooga. The twenty-nine states whose troops fought here have erected more than 600 monuments, 700 cast-iron markers (blue signifies Union actions, red Confederate troop movements), and 250 artillery pieces to mark significant sites on the battlefield. Large triangular mounds of cannonballs signify the locations where eight brigade commanders died; smaller ones mark the sites of army and corps headquarters; and acorn-topped monuments represent the positions occupied by the Fourteenth Corps, which stood solid as an oak tree with Thomas at Snodgrass Hill. Because the South could ill afford memorials after the war, most of the monuments in the park were erected by northern states. For example, Illinois has 143; Alabama has 1.

The battlefield is bisected by U.S. 27 (which is the LaFayette Road along which the armies battled). Fortunately, the highway will soon be rerouted.

The beautiful old visitors center (built in 1935) occupies the site where a log cabin stood at the time of the battle. Beside it is a new facility that features exhibits and a 150-seat auditorium with a 180-

degree panoramic screen 70 feet long and 13 feet high. The twenty-four-minute multimedia presentation employs forty-three slide projectors, thirteen hundred slides, five video players, and seven stereo speakers. It effectively enhances an understanding of the battle and subsequent actions around Chattanooga. A special feature is the Fuller Collection of American Military Shoulder Arms—an impressive display of 355 infantry weapons, forming a tangible history of American firearms with an emphasis on Civil War rifles. The collection was donated in 1954 by Claude E. and Zenada O. Fuller. Note the Sharps 1863 carbine with a coffee mill in the stock. A restored battery wagon and traveling forge are also displayed. An outdoor artillery park displays different types of ordnance used during the Civil War. Volunteer reenactors demonstrate cannon and rifle firing regularly.

Miles of roads and footpaths crisscross the large battlefield, and park officials have mapped out an easy-to-follow seven-mile automobile tour. A two-hour, twelve-mile audiotape-guided auto tour is also available.

The first of eight featured stops is Reed's Bridge. Forrest captured the span intact late on September 18 from Union Col. Robert H. G. Minty's cavalry. Confederate forces were then able to move into the area and initiate the early morning combat along three miles of the LaFayette Road as Bragg tried to turn Rosecrans's left flank and cut off the Federals' communications with Chattanooga.

Stop Two is the Kelly Farm, where Union forces erected log works and from which Rosecrans had sent substantial reinforcements on September 20 to Thomas to stave off Bragg. Polk attacked late and sacrificed his men to the massed Federals. The road here follows the Union position and is now lined with a large number of monuments. The Confederate line was to the east.

Stop Three describes the erroneous report of the nonexistent gap. Stop Four is the original Brotherton Cabin, where Rosecrans shifted an entire division to fill the fictional hole. Other divisions had yet to cover the real gap this caused in the Union lines when Longstreet attacked through the breach, routing two Federal divisions, fragmenting three more, and breaking Rosecrans's right flank. It was the most successful attack in the short history of the Confederacy. The imposing Georgia Monument—with figures representing infantry, artillery, and cavalry—is across the road.

Stop Five is the Viniard Field, which explains the terrible slaughter of September 19 as additional units were fed into the grinder and little territory changed hands. The charge and counter-charge were standup combat at its grisliest. The armies lost nearly a third of their strength here: 18,300 casualties for Bragg, 16,600 for Rosecrans. Only Gettysburg was more costly in the Civil War. The area is a forest of monuments, markers, and artillery.

The Wilder Tower at Stop Six, eighty-five-feet tall and con-structed of Chickamauga limestone, has a spiral staircase leading to an observation tower for a panoramic view of the battlefield. Erected by Col. John Wilder's veterans in 1899, it honors their mounted cavalry that slowed Longstreet's juggernaut with seven-shot repeaters and bought time for Thomas to mount a defense. Here was Rosecrans's headquarters of the previous day at the home of Mrs. Eliza Camp Glenn; her husband had been killed earlier in the war. The home burned during the battle, and Mrs. Glenn was left destitute to care for two infants, one born after her husband's death.

Stop Seven describes the rout of the Union left as tens of thou-sands of Federals fled to Chattanooga through McFarlan Gap.

Thomas's heroic stand is commemorated on Snodgrass Hill, where the Snodgrass Cabin has been recreated at Stop Eight. His one remaining division and portions of others threw up stone-and-log barricades and repulsed numerous determined attacks with the rein-forcements and ammunition brought by Granger, whose unordered appearance seemed divinely inspired. At dark, with the Army of the Cumberland safely gone, Thomas's forces melted away to join Rose-crans.

Also found in the park are impressive monuments erected by Florida, Texas, Alabama, South Carolina, Maryland, and Kentucky honoring sons who fought in both armies. Two large stones pay homage to Georgia units that fought at Chickamauga, the Thirty-seventh and the Forty-seventh Infantry.

The only marked grave on the field is near Alexander Bridge Road. Georgia Pvt. John Ingram was a friend of the local Reed family; they buried him and cared for the plot. *Chickamauga National Military Park is nine miles south of Chattanooga on U.S. 27, P.O. Box 2128, Fort Oglethorpe, GA 30742 (706) 866-9241.*

At Chickamauga's Snodgrass Hill, Federal Gen. George W. Thomas made a heroic stand to slow the Confederate onslaught.

Chickamauga Area

McFarlan Gap

This pass through which Rosecrans fled to Chattanooga is north of the Chickamauga visitors center on McFarlan Gap Road, off U.S. 27. Thomas Crittenden's corps crossed the Tennessee River at Shellmound, Tennessee, and advanced from Chattanooga via Rossville and this gap to Crawfish Springs.

Rossville

The two-story log John Ross House (1797) was built by a prominent Cherokee chief. It served as headquarters for Rosecrans's reserves, led by Granger. Open to the public, it is off U.S. 27 on East Lake Drive. *John Ross House Association, P.O. Box 863, Rossville, GA 30741 (706) 861-3954.*

At the Georgia state line on U.S. 27 is the Iowa Reservation, marked by a large monument, part of Chattanooga National Park. The Chattanooga National Battlefield is broken into small parcels of land called reservations, mostly in Tennessee on Missionary Ridge and Lookout Mountain. The Iowa Reservation, where Union troops began the start up Missionary Ridge, is in Georgia.

Fort Oglethorpe

Along U.S. 27, the Tennessee Cavalry Monument is in downtown Fort Oglethorpe. A new feature is an electronic map of the battle of Chickamauga at Battlerama, a series of multimedia displays of the many phases of the engagement. *GA 2, Fort Oglethorpe, GA 30742 (706) 866-5771.*

Chickamauga Village

The famous Gordon-Lee Mansion (1847), a twelve-room brick Greek Revival, and its grounds were used as Rosecrans's headquarters before the battle (September 16–19) and hosted seven Federal divisional hospitals during the fighting, one inside and six on the grounds. Surgeries were performed in many of the rooms, and wagons were placed beneath the windows for amputated limbs. After the Federals retreated, thirty army doctors remained to tend their wounded. The restored mansion is open now as a bed and breakfast inn. Across from the house is Crawfish Springs, where Union troops marching to battle stopped to fill their canteens. *Gordon-Lee Mansion, 217 Cove Road, Chickamauga, GA 30707 (706) 375-4729.*

After a Federal artillery battery deployed on the grounds of the nearby Hunt House, one shot flew through an open back door, penetrated two interior doors, a piece of furniture, and the front door. *Follow the signs to Chickamauga Village from U.S. 27 west of Chickamauga National Park.*

Gordon-Lee Mill. The first mill established on this site was built in 1836 by James Gordon. His son-in-law, James Morgan Lee, operated the mill when Confederate Gen. Leonidas Polk established his headquarters here when sent by Bragg to destroy Crittenden's isolated corps before the battle. Polk dallied, and the chance was lost. Crittenden used the mill as his headquarters for several days, forcing Lee to mill for the Federals. The building was between the lines during the battle and constant skirmishing occurred around it. The mill burned in 1867 but was rebuilt. It has not been used for many years and is not open to visitors. *Southwest of Chickamauga National Park off U.S. 27 on Lee and Gordon Mill Road.*

Walker County

LaFayette

Walker County's Civil War history began in September 1863 when Rosecrans advanced into Georgia. Bragg established his headquarters in LaFayette and turned to destroy Rosecrans, but Confederate Gen. D. H. Hill missed the chance to destroy Thomas's twenty-thousand-man corps as the Federals crossed narrow Stevens Gap over Lookout Mountain and marched into confined McLemore Cove. On the night of September 17 the Union army camped near the antebellum Cedar Grove Methodist Church.

In June 1864, 450 Union soldiers were quartered at the old courthouse in LaFayette when a Confederate cavalry force of 1,000 troopers launched a surprise attack at 3 A.M. The outnumbered Federals fought desperately and managed to hold off the Southerners until reinforcements arrived to repulse the attackers.

While drawing Sherman away from Atlanta in October 1864, Confederate Gen. John B. Hood established a defensive arc around LaFayette. The Union army concentrated against Hood, but the Confederate leader would not be engaged and withdrew into Alabama.

Gordon Hall. Erected in 1836, this two-story red-brick Georgian structure served as a school until 1920. Named for John B. Gordon, an outstanding Confederate general and state politician who lived nearby and attended the school as a child, the building is on the National Register of Historic Places. Tradition holds that Bragg planned the battle of Chickamauga under an oak tree out front while keeping his headquarters here September 16–19, 1863. The famed Bragg Oak was destroyed by lightning in 1920. Used as Union head-

Gordon Hall in LaFayette was Braxton Bragg's headquarters when he planned the battle of Chickamauga.

quarters in 1864, Gordon Hall was in the line of fire during the fighting in LaFayette. Originally there was a wooden annex, but it was torn down during the battle and used to build barricades. A Confederate monument—dedicated April 27, 1909, to tunes played by Fort Oglethorpe's Eleventh U.S. Cavalry Band—and a stack of cannonballs that marks the site of Bragg's headquarters are on the grounds. Gordon Hall is owned by the city. *On U.S. 27 (Main Street) in LaFayette.*

LaFayette Presbyterian Church. This brick church (1848) was used as a field hospital by both armies. Surgeries were performed outside on tables and inside on planks laid across the pews. The Confederate dead were buried in the LaFayette Cemetery at the end of Wardlaw, off U.S. 27. A monument to them stands just inside the grounds.

During the battle of LaFayette, Union and Confederate cavalrymen are said to have ridden through the Marsh-Warthen House (1836). Another legend claims that it was here that Bragg planned his strategy for Chickamauga while his men camped on the grounds outside. Bullet holes, hoof marks, and bloodstains remain on the walls and floor. *Open by appointment; 308 North Main Street, LaFayette, GA 30728 (706) 638-8944.*

Much of the battle occurred outside the Culberson-Burney House (Grace Manor, 1830s), which became a hospital with the overflow from the Presbyterian church. The Marsh Building (on the town square, 1838) and the Phillips-Stiles House (305 West Culberson Street, 1836) all have bullet scars from the combat in the streets. Both were used as hospitals following the battle.

Stevens Gap

Thomas crossed the Tennessee River at Bridgeport, Tennessee, and marched his corps through Rising Fawn and Trenton in Dade County and east into Johnson's Crook to cross Lookout Mountain via scenic Stevens Gap on GA 136, west of LaFayette, and into McLemore Cove. He withdrew along the same path before the disorganized Confederates could strike. McLemore Cove is along GA 193 between Lookout Mountain and Missionary Ridge to the west and Pigeon Mountain to the east. A skirmish was fought at Davis Crossroads, near the intersection of GA 193 and Hogjowl Road. Dug Gap, through which Confederate forces marched over Pigeon Mountain in an attempt to strike the Federals, is west of LaFayette on GA 193.

Chattooga County

On September 11, 1863, Union Gen. Daniel McCook's corps crossed the Tennessee River at Caperton's Ferry, Alabama, and threaded its way between Sand and Raccoon Mountains to cross Lookout Mountain at Valley Head, Alabama, via Winston Gap, to reach Alpine, two miles south of Menlo, between Pigeon Mountain and Taylor Ridge. Skirmishes occurred as they approached Summerville, forty-two miles south of Stevens Gap. The valleys were illuminated by hundreds of campfires on the ridges. Finding himself nearly isolated from the other Federal columns, McCook withdrew and followed Thomas to Chickamauga.

Many Unionists lived in this area and hid from the Home Guard in caves. Only walls of large stone blocks remain from the home of James Cooper Nisbit (1858), a Georgia Secessionist from Macon and a Confederate colonel who wrote a witty account of his war experiences. Hood marched his army through here in October 1864 on his way to Alabama.

Chattooga's only war monument stands, not at the county seat of Summerville, but in tiny Menlo. It is the only known cast-iron soldier statue and resembles granite until seen up close. It was erected in Lawrence Park by Andrew J. Lawrence, an interesting man and the town founder. His brother John enlisted in the Union army and was killed in action. Andrew joined the Confederate army but soon deserted and took the oath of allegiance to the Union. This monument was erected in compliance with his will. As befits his ambiguous position during the conflict, the inscription reads: To the private soldier of the Sixties.

McPherson's Flanking Movements. At the beginning of the Atlanta campaign in May 1864, Federal Gen. William T. Sherman intended to flank Confederate Gen. Joseph E. Johnston out of a strong position in Dalton by sending Gen. James B. McPherson's Army of the Tennessee through Snake Creek Gap and south to Resaca. McPherson skirted the old Chickamauga battlefield on the present route of U.S. 27, turned east on GA 95 at Rock Springs, moved south on GA 151 at Chestnut Flat, camping there the night of May 7, going east on GA 136 through Maddox Gap over Taylor's Ridge to seize Villanow and marching through beautiful Snake Creek Gap between Mill Creek and Horn Mountains to emerge at Resaca. When Hood withdrew to LaFayette in October 1864, closely pursued by Sherman, he blocked the gap with felled timber.

County Road (CR) 1030 runs the length of scenic West Armuchee Valley between Taylor's Ridge and Dick's Ridge to Shiloh Church, where Hood's leg was amputated following the battle at Chickamauga.

Confederate Works. Atop thirteen-hundred-foot-high Dick's Ridge is a long stone wall that was probably used as a Confederate fortification. It is at the end of Chickamauga Creek Trail, a four-mile-round-trip hike. *About 3.5 miles west of Villanow, off Powder Creek Road and Forest Service Road 219-a.* (A Chattahoochee National Forest map is available from the U.S. Forest Service.)

Rome

The city of Rome was an important industrial center for the Confederacy, providing desperately needed iron and munitions. In 1863 Federal Col. A. D. Streight led two thousand cavalry on a raid to destroy Rome's industrial capacity. He was foiled by John H. Wisdom, who rode eighty-seven miles in eight hours from Gadsden, Alabama, through Cave Springs and Vann's Valley to Rome to warn of the approaching enemy. Farmers and convalescents barricaded the streets with cotton bales and readied to destroy the bridges. Nathan Bedford Forrest pursued Streight with only five hundred men and tricked the entire Union force into surrendering in eastern Alabama. Forrest was honored in Rome on May 3, 1863.

In 1864 Sherman dispatched Gen. Jefferson C. Davis's division from Resaca to capture Rome, preceded by Gen. Kenner Garrard's cavalry. Garrard started on May 15, moving through Villanow to camp at Floyd Springs, then continued to Farmers Bridge (Armuchee) where he skirmished with Confederate cavalry and crossed the creek at the U.S. 27 bridge, continuing to DeSoto Hill on the east bank of the Oostanaula River near U.S. 27. Davis reached DeSoto Hill on May 17, skirmished again, and crossed the following day to capture the city as Confederate forces under Maj. Gen. Samuel G. French withdrew, burning the bridges and evacuating five hilltop forts. Rome was garrisoned until November 10 when the Federals abandoned the city as Sherman marched to Savannah, first destroying Rome's factories, commercial establishments, several homes, and other private property.

Myrtle Hill Cemetery. Rome's Civil War attractions are concentrated in this historic cemetery. A monument to Floyd County's Confederate soldiers was erected on Confederate Memorial Day 1887. It was first topped with an urn, and twenty years later a soldier figure was erected during a ceremony featuring fifteen hundred schoolchildren. The statue resembled a Spanish-American War Rough Rider and was replaced later. On May 3, 1908, a statue of Nathan Bedford Forrest was dedicated. A particularly moving monument, unveiled on March 9, 1910, honors the women of the Confederacy. One side of the monument depicts a kneeling woman attending to the needs of a wounded soldier; on the opposite side a woman tells

Confederate soldiers who died in Rome's hospitals are buried on a hillside in Myrtle Hill Cemetery.

a little girl how her father died in battle. The inscription was written by Woodrow Wilson, whose first wife is buried here. Both monuments were relocated from their original sites on Broad Street.

One plot contains the graves of 377 Confederates and 2 Federals who died in Rome hospitals and in skirmishes around the area. John Wisdom, the "Confederate Paul Revere," is also buried here. A walking brochure guide of Myrtle Hill Cemetery is available from the Rome Convention and Visitors Bureau. *At South Broad Street (U.S. 27) and Myrtle Street in Rome.*

Noble Foundry Lathe. The foundry produced ship engines, locomotives, and seventy cannon for the Confederacy until it was destroyed in November 1864 by Sherman's withdrawing forces. An enormous machine manufactured in 1847 in New Hampshire, it has survived and is now preserved as a monument. The lathe was too large to be transported by railroad, so it was sent by sea to Mobile, up the Alabama and Coosa Rivers to the falls, then disassembled and hauled by ox cart to the city. The Federals found it too massive and solid to be destroyed and were forced to leave it intact. Scars from sledgehammer blows are still evident. It had been used in the manufacture of cannon and remained in use through the 1960s. A

This enormous lathe was used in the manufacture of cannon for the Confederacy.

Corliss steam engine stands beside the equipment, the type used to power the lathe. *The Noble Brothers Foundry and Machine Shop stood at Broad Street and First Avenue; the lathe is beside the Rome Visitors Center, 402 Civic Center Drive, Rome, GA 30161 (706) 295-5576; (800) 444-1834.*

On the hill behind the Rome visitors center are the remains of Fort Norton, Rome's primary defensive structure during the Civil War. The earthwork is in an excellent state of preservation and there are plans to restore it. A monument on West Thirteenth Street honors Texans who defended Rome and marks the site of Fort Stovall.

Chieftains Museum (1794). On the National Register, Chieftains was the home of Cherokee leader Major Ridge. Preserved by the

Junior Service League as a city museum, it houses exhibits of Rome's Civil War importance. *501 Riverside Parkway Northeast, between GA Spur 57 and U.S. 27; P.O. Box 373, Rome, GA 30162-0373 (706) 291-9494.*

Federals camped on the grounds of beautiful Oak Hill (1847), home of famed educator Martha Berry. Its outbuildings were destroyed during the occupation. *U.S. 27 North and GA Loop 1, Box 189, Mount Berry Station, GA 30194-0189 (706) 291-1883.*

A monument honoring the Union soldiers who captured Rome is on West Thirteenth Street. The present Masonic Temple (1877) was built with contributions from Federals who, not knowing it was a lodge, had burned the original in 1864. Gen. Jefferson C. Davis occupied the demolished Rose Hill, home of Maj. Charles H. Smith, the famed postwar writer known as Bill Arp. Sherman stayed in the home twice, on October 12 and between October 28 and November 2, while chasing Hood into Alabama and organizing plans for his March to the Sea respectively. Thornwood (1848), west of Rome, was occupied by an advance force of two hundred troops from Streight's command under Capt. Milton Russell, who was to secure the bridges over the Oostanaula River. They failed in their mission due to Wisdom's warning and were captured. The First Presbyterian Church (101 East Third Street [706] 291-6033, 1849) was used as a hospital, and the Methodist Episcopal church (now Saint Paul's African Methodist Episcopal Church, Sixth Avenue and West Second Street [706] 232-4807, 1852) was used as a Union stable.

Emma Sansom was born in 1848 near Social Circle, Georgia. Her family moved in 1855 to Etowah County, Alabama, bordering Floyd County, Georgia. On May 2, 1863, the family watched Federal cavalry fire the bridge over Black Creek to slow the unrelenting pursuit of Forrest's cavalry. When the famed commander appeared and asked the Sansoms about fording the rain-swollen stream, Emma knew of a place where cattle crossed, and Forrest swung her into the saddle with him. During the pursuit the Federals fired on the advancing Forrest, sending a bullet through Emma's skirts, but they chivalrously ceased fire when she waved her bonnet at them. Forrest crossed the stream and stopped Streight before he could enter Georgia.

The Confederate Congress thanked Emma with a gold medal. The state of Alabama gave her 640 acres in 1899, and in 1907 the UDC erected a life-sized statue of her at the courthouse in Gadsden, Alabama. A stone marker stands at the creek crossing. Emma married a Confederate veteran and moved to Tyler, Texas, where she is buried.

Cave Spring

Ninety historic structures survive in this orderly village nestled in Vann's Valley. In October 1864 Hood met here with his superior, Gen. P. G. T. Beauregard, to discuss the future operations of the Army of Tennessee. The original administration buildings of the Georgia School for the Deaf (1846) were used as hospitals for both armies. The school was closed for the duration of the war, opening again in 1867.

The buildings of the school (which moved in 1973) and the spring in a cave for which the community is noted are in Rolater Park on the Cedartown Road (Old GA 100). The Turner Home (mid-1800s) was occupied by Federals.

Polk County

During Sherman's shift from Kingston to Dallas, McPherson's army swung far west and marched through eastern Polk County, following Euharlee Creek to Aragon, where they camped at Peek's Spring. On the following day the Federals turned east through Van Wert and marched on to Dallas. On October 26, 1906, a Confederate monument was erected on the courthouse lawn in Cedartown; Kilpatrick had burned the earlier courthouse and sixty-five other downtown buildings.

Carroll County

In April 1865 part of Union Gen. James Wilson's cavalry passed through Carrollton. The county was raided four times by Federal foraging parties. On the courthouse square is a Confederate statue, dedicated April 26, 1910, to Carroll County's Southern veterans.

Haralson County

Surviving Federal cavalrymen from the Brown's Mill disaster near Newnan circled through Alabama and reached the Union lines at Marietta by way of Buchanan and Draketown.

The West Georgia Museum has exhibits of Civil War artifacts, maps, etc. *21 West Lyon Street, P.O. Box 725, Tallapoosa, GA 30176 (770) 574-3125.*

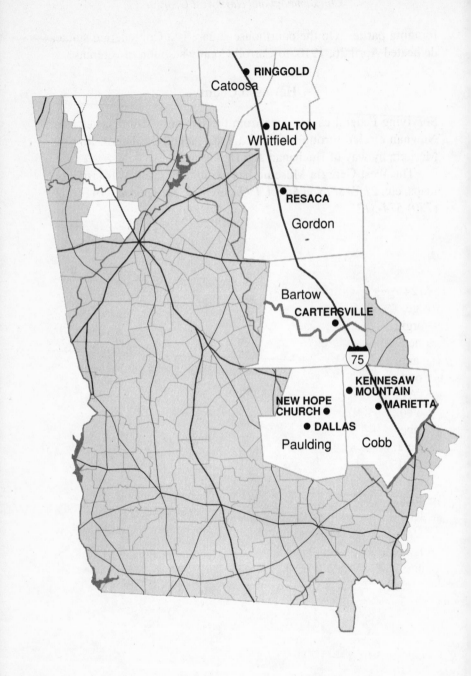

2

The Atlanta Campaign

A FTER CHICKAMAUGA, Bragg besieged Chattanooga and attempted to starve Rosecrans into surrender. The strategy might have worked, but Union Gens. Ulysses S. Grant and William T. Sherman arrived from Mississippi with massive reinforcements. On November 24–25, following battles at Lookout Mountain and Missionary Ridge, the Confederates were thrown back in disarray to Dalton, Georgia. Federal strategy now called for the capture of Atlanta, one of the South's few remaining industrial centers, and a strike on either Savannah or Mobile, Alabama, that would split the Confederacy a second time.

As Grant departed to engage Lee in Virginia, he appointed Sherman commander of the western armies—the mammoth Army of the Cumberland under George W. Thomas, James B. McPherson's Army of the Tennessee, and John Schofield's Army of the Ohio—totaling more than one hundred thousand men. On the Confederate side, Bragg resigned and was replaced by Joseph E. Johnston. His fifty-thousand-man Army of Tennessee was divided into three corps under John B. Hood, William J. Hardee, and Leonidas Polk.

Johnston established a strong defensive position on the mountains north and west of Dalton. Sherman intended to demonstrate against Dalton while a third of his army moved to outflank Johnston through the shielded mountain passes.

Catoosa County

Great Locomotive Chase. A stone monument marking the place where the chase ended is on GA 151 beside the railroad, two miles

31

north of Ringgold. James J. Andrews and his raiders scattered into the woods but were captured. (*See page 57.*)

Just to the north in Graysville is the Gray Home, spared by Sherman because the owner was a Mason. Federal troops were stationed on the grounds, and Grant used the structure as a headquarters. To the west, on GA 820, is Ellis Spring, where Union cavalry under Col. Robert H. G. Minty fired on Confederate horsemen. The skirmish continued to Reed's Bridge, which the Federals did not have sufficient time to torch. Shots fired there on September 16, 1863, are considered the beginning of the battle of Chickamauga. Southwest, at the Daniel Majors House, Union guerrillas seized Majors, and he was never seen again. The Stage Coach House at New Echota and Crawfish Springs Roads and the Napier House were both used as hospitals during the battle of Chickamauga.

Ringgold

Old Stone Depot. The depot was built along the Western and Atlantic Railroad in 1849 with local sandstone and remained in use until recent decades. When the Confederates were routed from their siege of Chattanooga, an avenue into the heart of the Confederacy seemed open, but Irish-born Confederate Gen. Patrick Cleburne fought a desperate rear-guard action in Ringgold Gap on November 25 to prevent the Federals from destroying Bragg's retreating army, an action that earned him the Thanks of Congress (Confederate). The depot was damaged by artillery fire in this action, and its repairs with lighter colored blocks are easy to detect at the roofline and southern end. In May 1864 Sherman occupied Ringgold to begin his drive on Atlanta. *On U.S. 41 (Nashville Street) at the southern edge of Ringgold.*

The present courthouse (1939) is the third on the site. The original courthouse (1854) was spared by Union soldiers because it also housed a Masonic hall. The Baptist and Presbyterian churches, still on their original sites, served as hospitals. The Methodist church, no longer on its original site, was financed by Northern congregations. Other hospitals operated in hotels and warehouses with nursing staffs supplemented with the women of the area, a situation common throughout Georgia. The hospitals were evacuated farther south in September 1863 as the Federals approached.

A family watched the Ringgold battle rage in the streets from the second floor of the Whitman-Anderson House (309 Tennessee Street, 1850s), and Grant used the home. Legend holds that the lady of the house demanded Confederate currency when Grant offered her U.S. dollars. The general commented, "She certainly is not whipped yet." The Felker House also witnessed the battle. At the corner of Nashville and Guyler Streets is the Evans House, a boarding home for female nurses working in the hospitals.

Ringgold Atlanta Campaign Pavilion. During the 1930s the Works Project Administration (WPA) built a series of roadside stations, mainly along U.S. 41, the primary north-south thoroughfare, to acquaint travelers with the Atlanta campaign. Designed by John Steinichen, the cost of the project was $127,000, and the bronze markers were cast at Georgia Tech. Each of the five circular field-stone pavilions contains a historical marker that describes the military importance of the area, a large metal relief map that illustrates the movements of the armies, and picnic facilities. Behind the pavilion is a trail leading through the woods and across the railroad tracks to a large granite monument with bronze plaques at the site where Col. John Ireland's New York Brigade fought. *On U.S. 41 one-half mile south of the Old Stone Depot.*

Old Stone Church. This beautiful church has stood since 1850 when it was built of stone quarried from a nearby mountain. It was used as a hospital following the fighting at Ringgold Gap; bloodstains remain on the floor and bullets are still embedded in the walls. The altar and pews are original. *On U.S. 41 three miles south of Ringgold.*

The Atlanta campaign began several miles east of Ringgold near Lee's Chapel on GA 2, where Sherman, Thomas, and Schofield observed their troops advancing on Dalton. Thomas followed GA 151, west of Taylor's Ridge, camping on May 6 at Pleasant Grove Church, Peavine Church, and Leet's Tanyard, which had been Bragg's quarters during the battle of Chickamauga. State Road (SR) 192-326 crosses Taylor's Ridge at Nickajack Gap where Thomas crossed, approaching Dalton through Trickum. West of GA 201 on Dunnagan Road near Liberty Church in Dogwood Valley is the Anderson House, Union

Gen. Joseph Hooker's headquarters at Dalton. Schofield's army was to the east at Tunnel Hill and Crow Valley.

Catoosa Station is in the area; Bragg's headquarters was in the freight room. Because the bridges farther north had been burned, Longstreet had disembarked here to march to Chickamauga and win the battle on the following day, September 18.

This region boasted many mineral spring resorts before the Civil War. On SR 388 to the east in Cherokee Valley was Cherokee Springs, used as a Confederate hospital and where Bragg and his wife were treated. It contained five hundred beds, as did Catoosa Springs, Georgia's finest prewar resort, farther east on GA 2. Cavalry skirmishes swept across the grounds. The buildings have vanished, but the springs are maintained in a scenic setting on private land. A saltpeter cave that supplied material for manufacturing gunpowder is now closed.

Whitfield County

Tunnel Hill

The railroad tunnel (1850), 1,477 feet long, required twenty-two months to excavate through Chetoogeta Ridge. A Confederate camp was maintained here through the winter and spring of 1864 to prevent Federal raids. When Sherman arrived in mid-1864 the Confederates skirmished briefly atop the ridge and then retreated.

The *General* had raced through the tunnel in 1862, followed by the backward-traveling *Texas*. Inside the tunnel, four alcoves were prepared for pedestrians to use when they encountered approaching trains. In 1928 a replacement tunnel was opened beside it. The Georgia General Assembly has deeded the land containing the tunnel to the city of Tunnel Hill for restoration and development as an interpretive park. It is dangerous to enter in its present state—bricks fall easily from the ceiling. *In downtown Tunnel Hill, south of Oak Street at the railroad. The original stone depot is beside the tracks.*

The Clisby Austin House (Meadowland), originally built as a resort hotel, is on Clisby Austin Road beside the railroad. John Bell Hood recuperated here following the loss of his leg at Chickamauga. The limb, which accompanied him so it could be buried with him should he die of infection, is in the family cemetery. The Unionist owner offered the house as Sherman's headquarters during the Dalton operation. Wisely he moved after the Federals withdrew lest his neighbors retaliate. In the mid-1980s a horror movie, *Offspring*, was filmed here depicting Southern orphans witnessing the execution of Confederates then seizing a Union officer and burning him at the stake. The Foster House, at Jordan and Cherry Streets, was used as a Civil War hospital.

Dalton

Dalton Atlanta Campaign Pavilion. The marker and map tell of Sherman's unsuccessful assaults in Mill Creek Gap, east at Crow Valley, and south at Dug Gap. It concludes by noting his successful flanking maneuver that caused Johnston's retreat south to Resaca during May 7–13, 1864. Confederate works commanded the ridge behind and across the highway, and the creek was damned to create a water barrier. Directly north is Blue Mountain, where Sherman oversaw the movement of his troops. Much of Dalton was destroyed during the Union occupation. *Beneath the State Patrol Post in Mill Creek Gap, on U.S. 41 at the northern edge of Dalton.*

Crow Valley. The Confederate defensive works began at Rocky Face to the west, stretched across the valley, and ended at Potato Top, a large hill to the northeast where Confederate artillery helped repulse the Federal attack. Schofield advanced from Red Clay, Tennessee—a Northern supply depot and now a Tennessee state park honoring Cherokee Indians—through Cohutta, Varnell, and Harris Gap. The valley is also noted as the execution site of a number of deserters shortly after Johnston assumed command of the Army of Tennessee. *On Crow Valley Road, east of U.S. 41-GA 3 via Willowdale Road.*

Westview (or West Hill) Cemetery. Buried here are 421 unknown and 4 known Confederate soldiers and 4 unknown Federals who died in Dalton hospitals of battle wounds or disease suffered in Tennessee or at Chickamauga. A small monument was erected in memory of the unknown dead, and a larger one, topped by the statue of a Confederate soldier, honors the Southerners who fought in the area. Gen. Bryan M. Thomas (1836–1905), West Point class of 1858, is interred here. He fought with the Army of Tennessee and ended the war in Mobile. *In Westview (or West Hill) Cemetery on Emory in Dalton.*

Joseph Johnston Statue. An impressive bronze statue of Johnston stands at the intersection of Crawford and Hamilton in downtown Dalton. Executed by Nashville native Belle Kinney, it was dedicated on October 24, 1912. Johnston commanded in Virginia prior to Robert E. Lee's being given command of the Army of Northern Virginia and twice led the Army of Tennessee. Unlike other lionized Virginia generals, this is his only monument.

Crown Gardens and Archives, Whitfield-Murray Historical Society. The archives include an exhibit of Civil War material, some excavated on the grounds from camps of the Orphan Brigade. Records of local Civil War units are on file. *715 Chattanooga Avenue, Dalton, GA 30720 (706) 278-0217.*

Western and Atlantic Depot (1852). On April 4, 1862, railroaders in pursuit of Andrews's raiders and the stolen *General* dropped off a telegraph boy to alert Chattanooga of the threat. Longstreet's troops also passed through here en route to Chickamauga and were met with cheers and food by local residents. These men were soon followed by casualty trains. Johnston disembarked here to take command of the Army of Tennessee. The depot remained in service until 1978 and is now a restaurant. *110 East Depot Street.*

Dug Gap Battlefield Park. This narrow pass was one of three routes into Dalton over rugged Rocky Face Ridge that Sherman attempted to storm. The Confederates established a strong line of stone breastworks across the summit of the mountain and easily repelled a determined Union attack on May 8. In a famous episode of the war, the defenders levered huge boulders down the steep slope that crashed through advancing Federal lines with demoralizing effect. A 1,237-foot section of the stone wall has been preserved along a footpath. *On Dug Gap Battle Road, atop Rocky Face Ridge, two miles west of I-75 (706) 278-0217.*

At the northern end of the ridge is the isolated grave of George Disney, a Kentucky private posted there when Thomas's forces probed Dalton's defenses on February 25, 1864. Killed by a stray shot, he was buried beneath a wooden marker. Boy Scouts rediscovered the grave in 1911, and a stone monument was erected.

Below and to the west is Mill Creek Valley. Union Gen. John W. Geary deployed his batteries at Babb's Settlement (Mill Creek Road at Hurricane Road) to assault Dug Gap.

The Huff House (314 Selvidge Street, 1850s) was Johnston's headquarters during the winter of 1864. A tent on the grounds of the Hamilton House (701 Chattanooga Avenue, 1846) was the headquarters of Brig. Gen. John H. Lewis of Kentucky's famed Orphan Brigade. The house was a hospital for both armies until the end of the war, and troops camped around Big Spring.

The family abandoned the Blunt House (506 South Thorton Avenue, 1843) and moved to Illinois for the duration of the war. Federals used the house and grounds for a hospital, covering the yard with temporary shelters called brush arbors. The U.S. government later compensated the Blunt family $1,815 for damages. *Tours are arranged through Crown Gardens and Archives ([706] 278-0217).*

Sherman constructed a blockhouse atop Fort Hill to protect the city; Hood captured it in October 1864.

The walls of the Varnell House (1847), at the intersection of GA 2 and GA 201, are still marked with bullets embedded from cavalry skirmishes on the grounds. The house was used as a hospital by both sides and as headquarters by several Union generals. On May 12, 1864, Confederate Gen. Joseph "Fighting Joe" Wheeler commanded a raid here around the Union left flank and inflicted 150 casualties, taking 100 prisoners.

Praters Mill (1855). On February 23, 1864, six hundred soldiers under Col. Eli Long camped here while Thomas moved against Dalton. On April 13, twenty-five hundred Confederate cavalry under Wheeler occupied the grounds of this three-story gristmill. Festivals are held here each spring and fall. *GA 2 ten miles northeast of Dalton, 808 Shugart Road, Dalton, GA 30720 (706) 275-6455.*

Walnut Grove. On Five Springs Road eight miles south of Dalton, this house was used as a Union headquarters and hospital. Patients carved their names on a closet, and residents saved the house by painting a large American flag on the roof.

Tilton

In 1862 the *General* stopped here for wood and water. Sherman's pursuit of Johnston was hampered here by a sharp rear-guard action. Federals later built a blockhouse here to protect the railroad. It was attacked on October 13, 1864, by Hood, whose artillery blasted it into capitulation. Schofield's troops crossed the Conasauga River nearby at Hogan's Ford and the several ferries, including Fite's, camping at Old Holly Post Office in Murray County. Continuing south through Gordon County, they crossed the Coosawattee at Field's Ferry and McClure's Ferry and passed through Harlan's Crossroads, Redbud, Cash (camping beside Dew's Pond, where a beautiful stone mill remains), and Sonoraville. The Federals entered Bartow County at Mosteller's Mills, an early manufacturing center where some ruins remain on private land near GA 140 at Cedar Creek. The column continued through Pleasant Valley toward Cassville. *Tilton Road east of U.S. 41-GA 3, south of Dalton.*

Nance's Spring

On May 9, 1864, Union raiders slipped south of Johnston and cut the telegraph wires between Dalton and Atlanta at John H. Green's wood station, a fueling stop on the Western and Atlantic Railroad. Two local women, Miss Carrie Sims and her sister, Mrs. Bachman, became heroines for splicing the wires together, restoring Confederate communications.

Gordon County

Resaca

McPherson flanked Johnston out of Dalton and was given the task of cutting off the Confederate line of retreat to Resaca, but the Union general overestimated the defenders' strength and failed to attack. Johnston withdrew to prepare defensive works here as Sherman moved his army through Snake Creek Gap, precipitating the first full engagement of the Atlanta campaign on May 14–15. Several Federal attacks on the center of the Confederate line were decimated, and an assault on the Union left by Hood almost succeeded in turning Sherman's flank. Taking advantage of his superior numbers, Sherman crossed the Oostanaula River downstream at Lay's Ferry to again threaten Johnston's rear, forcing him to retire farther south.

Resaca Battlefield. This is the Camp Creek Valley, now cleared of trees and underbrush by construction work for I-75. Union forces occupied positions on the western ridge. Confederates controlled the eastern ridge, their line running north from the Conasauga then east to the river near the Confederate cemetery. The ridges were heavily wooded, and the valley became a slaughterhouse during repeated futile Federal assaults. Union troops hid until dark in the creek and then withdrew. Sherman approached Resaca via the gap on the western horizon from Snake Creek Gap. Here McPherson dislodged Polk from the ridge and bombarded the Confederate-controlled bridges over the river. Although some of the battlefield was destroyed by highway construction, much remains in private hands and may be preserved. *On GA 136 one-half mile west of U.S. 41 at the Camp Creek Bridge, facing north.*

Resaca Atlanta Campaign Pavilion. The marker and map describe Johnston's retreat from Dalton, the fighting at Resaca, and the Confederate withdrawal. At the northern corner is a monument commemorating the Resaca Confederate Cemetery. *On U.S. 41 one mile south of the Dalton–Gordon County line.*

Confederate Cemetery. After the battle Miss Mary J. Green organized the women in the area to move the Confederate dead from the battlefield to this site. More than 420 unknown soldiers are buried in circles around a monument topped with a cross. Interred beside the soldiers is Mrs. E. J. Simmons, a leader in establishing the cemetery. A stone wall pierced by a high entrance arch surrounds the cemetery, and great oaks shade the quiet grounds. Services are faithfully held here each Confederate Memorial Day. *At the end of CR 97 one-half mile east of the Resaca Atlanta Campaign Pavilion.*

The county road immediately north leads to a natural amphitheater in the rolling hills where Hood nearly turned Sherman's left. Each May reenactments are held here. Earthworks survive on private property where Federals staged a daring night raid and seized four cannon Hood was forced to abandon.

Railroad Bridge. Still in use are the original supports of the Western and Atlantic Railroad, which Andrews's raiders crossed in 1862 through a covered bridge that had been their primary target. Closely pursued, Andrews tried to use two cars to slam into his pursuers, but the Confederates successfully coupled the cars to their backward-racing locomotive. East of the bridge are the remains of a Union earthwork intended to protect the span. It was so formidable that Hood chose not to attack it in October 1864. *Just east of U.S. 41 a mile south of Resaca.*

Calhoun

Confederate Monument. This unique memorial consists of an arch with the figure of a Confederate soldier standing on one side and a Doughboy from the First World War opposite. *At the intersection of U.S. 41 and GA 225 north of Calhoun.*

Oakleigh. Now the headquarters of the Gordon County Historical Society, Oakleigh is thought to have been used by Sherman as a temporary headquarters. *335 South Wall Street (U.S. 41), P.O. Box 342, Calhoun, GA 30701 (706) 829-1515.*

Calhoun is noted for two other incidents: Andrews nearly collided with a southbound passenger train here, and at Oothcaloga Creek on GA 53 to the west, Hardee delayed McPherson for a day. A brochure describing Civil War attractions from Chattanooga to Marietta is available on request by writing: Blue and Gray Trail, 300 South Wall Street, Calhoun, GA 30701 (706) 629-3406.

Bartow County

Adairsville

This community held a strategic importance since it was a terminus for the Western and Atlantic Railroad and housed a roundhouse, large machine shops, and a gunpowder and weapons factory. The Oothcaloga Valley was also one of Georgia's granaries. Here William A. Fuller secured the *Texas* to pursue Andrews's raiders and the *General.* Johnston established a temporary line to the north, but the ridges were too widely separated to be defensible. He then decided to split his army, half marching to Kingston, the other half to Cassville to trap Schofield. Much of the town was burned during the war. At the Old Courthouse (1884) on the public square is a monument to the Great Locomotive Chase. The depot is touted as the original that was involved in the chase. This event is celebrated in a festival each year.

McPherson marched to the west on May 17, camping at McGuire's, where GA 53 and 140 meet, and continuing the next day to Barnsley Gardens via scenic Snow Valley. He then camped west of Kingston at Wooley's Plantation, where buildings remain but are not open to the public. At Cassville, McPherson crossed the Etowah River and advanced toward Dallas via Macedonia Church while Thomas and Schofield used Gillem's Bridge and a pontoon span at Milam's Bridge.

Barnsley Gardens

In 1840 Godfrey Barnsley began his grand three-story, twenty-eight-room mansion, which he named Woodlands. As the Federals approached, Confederate Col. Richard G. Earle raced to warn his friend Barnsley of the approaching threat and was killed by Union soldiers as he left. His grave is a landmark on the grounds. Barnsley flew the British flag and claimed neutrality, despite the fact that his fortune was invested in Confederate bonds and his two sons fought for the Confederacy. McPherson issued orders that Woodlands not be harmed. When he departed on May 19, stragglers broke into the wine cellar and drank or destroyed two thousand bottles and then burned furniture and smashed statuary. Barnsley filed a claim for $155,000 in damages against the Federal government through the British consulate in Washington but collected nothing.

Barnsley lost his fortune—the bonds were worthless and two of his blockade-runners were lost—and his sons refused to take the oath of allegiance, so the family immigrated to the Confederate colony in Brazil. The house decayed over the years, and in 1906 a tornado took the roof. The ruins were rescued in the mid-1980s by investors who restored the extensive gardens, stabilized the impressive ruins, and opened a small museum with Civil War artifacts. *Barnsley Gardens at Woodlands, 597 Barnsley Gardens Road, Adairsville, GA 30103 (770) 733-7480.*

Kingston

Kingston hosted Sherman twice. On May 19, 1864, expecting Johnston to make a stand here, Sherman arrived to find the wily Confederate was instead at Cassville to the east, waiting to destroy an isolated portion of the Federal army. In November, after chasing Hood into Tennessee, Sherman paused several days in Kingston where he received Grant's permission to campaign against Savannah. He planned his devastating March to the Sea at the Thomas Van Buren Hargin House, which burned in 1947. Most of the town was torched when Sherman left. Thomas and McPherson followed Hardee here from Adairsville via Halls Station Road while Schofield marched to Cassville along the route of U.S. 41. Eight clashes between Union and Confederate cavalry occurred in the area between June and September 1864.

Kingston Park. Confederate Gen. William T. Wofford surrendered the last Confederate troops east of the Mississippi on May 12, 1865, in this large city park in the center of town. Federal Gen. Henry Judah fed and paroled the four thousand men, mostly Georgians. At the southern edge of the park is a monument stating that Kingston hosted eight Confederate hospitals and honoring the women who attended to the needs of ten thousand patients. The Methodist church facing the park was the only church here that survived Sherman, and it hosted all denominations for many years following the war. Its pastor was Confederate Gen. Clement Evans, who also gained renown as a historian of the Civil War. The Kingston Confederate Memorial Museum (13 East Main Street, Kingston, GA 30145 [770] 336-5269) is open by appointment.

Great Locomotive Chase. The *General* was delayed an hour by several passing trains, allowing Fuller to close the distance. Andrews raced the nine miles between Kingston and Adairsville in seven minutes.

Confederate Cemetery. In the city cemetery are the graves of 1 identified (Georgia Pvt. Sterling F. Chandler) and 249 unknown Confederate solders and 2 unknown Federals who died in the area hospitals. There is a small monument recognizing the unknown dead while a large obelisk honoring all the soldiers towers above the enclosure. Beside the plot is a memorial to Kingston's Confederate veterans who survived the war. Tradition holds that the first Confederate Memorial Day was held here in 1865 when Union Gen. Henry Judah allowed the women of the town to decorate the Confederate graves if they would also decorate the graves of any Federals. Observances continue to this day. *Johnson Street south of the park; Kingston is on GA 293 between Cassville and Adairsville.*

On May 18, 1864, Confederate and Federal armies marched past Spring Bank Plantation, between Kingston and Cassville, and Oliver O. Howard briefly occupied the house. The owner, the Reverend Charles H. Howard, ran an academy and raised the Sixty-third Georgia Infantry Regiment. At war's end, Generals Wofford and Judah met in the parlor to arrange surrender terms. The home burned in the 1970s, but the family cemetery contains the grave of Everett B. D. Julio, a French artist who painted *The Last Meeting of Lee and Jackson,* a famed painting prominently displayed at the Museum of the Confederacy in Richmond. The presence of the New Orleans painter is a mystery—it is claimed he taught at the school or was simply passing through when he fell ill with tuberculosis. He died in 1879 and is buried in a rock-lined grave surrounded by a wrought-iron fence.

Several plantation homes with Civil War histories can be found along Robert Stiles Road off Euharlee Road north of and overlooking the Etowah River near Euharlee. Valley View was the headquarters of the Union occupation commander, Gen. George W. Schofield, who remained for three months. The iron balcony railing was sent to Cooper's Iron Foundry for use in making bullets (this story is highly unlikely), and the piano was used as a trough.

While camped near Etowah Cliff at the William H. Stiles House, Union Gen. Milo S. Hascall wrote to Sherman describing the "wonton [*sic*] destruction of private property" committed by Federal soldiers. He had seen half a dozen homes burning at one time.

Popular myth holds that while Sherman was attending West Point, he courted and was rejected by Miss Cecelia Stovall, mistress of Shelman Heights (which burned in 1911) when the Union army passed through the area. She was not at home, but when Sherman discovered that this was her property, he ordered that the home not be burned. Beware romantic historic legends.

Etowah Valley resident Fanny Howard recounted her adventures here during the war in the book *In and Out of the Lines.*

Between Kingston and Gillem's Bridge on the Etowah River was the Bartow Saltpeter Works; saltpeter was used in gunpowder production at Augusta. Work crews of up to one hundred free workers and slaves brought out four hundred to one thousand pounds a day. Confederates destroyed the works on May 18, 1864, as they retreated. Other caves were mined in Cherokee and Chattooga Counties. The cave is marked but closed to the public, although organized cave exploration groups mount occasional tours.

Cassville

When Johnston was forced to retreat from Resaca, he sent the bulk of his army to Cassville while leading Sherman to believe that he had withdrawn to Kingston. Sherman sent Schofield's corps to Cassville with the hope that he would flank the Confederates out of Kingston. Seeing this, Johnston intended to annihilate Schofield. The plan was faultless, but the recalcitrant Hood failed to attack and the opportunity was lost. While Johnston established a position on a ridge south of Cassville, Sherman united his army on a ridge north of town. Johnston again planned to attack Sherman, but two of his

Cass Station marked the end of the Confederate battle line at Cassville.

corps commanders—Hood and Polk—claimed that the field was unfavorable, forcing Johnston to withdraw behind the Etowah River to a stronger position in the Allatoona Mountains.

Cassville was the seat of Cass County, boasting a population of two thousand, two colleges, and many fine homes and businesses. The area saw significant guerrilla activity, and after a captured Union patrol was murdered, Sherman ordered that every structure within five miles be burned, including Cassville. On a cold and rainy November 15, 1864, the citizens were given minutes to evacuate the town before it was torched. Only three churches and three homes, all of which served as hospitals, survived the fire, but the city was never rebuilt. Many residents died of hunger or exposure during the winter. The only surviving structures are the beautiful Methodist and Presbyterian churches and a WPA marker in a field that marks the old courthouse square.

Cassville Atlanta Campaign Pavilion. Although this is the largest of the five monuments, it has fallen into disrepair. Parts of the stone wall are collapsing, and the metal map has been stolen, but the historical marker remains to describe Johnston's failed attempt to trap Sherman. *On U.S. 41 three miles north of Cartersville.*

Confederate Cemetery. More than five hundred men died in Cassville's eight hospitals, but the bodies of two hundred were claimed by relatives. The remaining three hundred—only one of whose identity is known (W. M. Barrow of Louisiana)—were buried together on this hillside in the city cemetery. In 1878 a tall obelisk, similar to Kingston's, was erected by the Ladies Memorial Association to honor the soldiers' sacrifice. Headstones were placed by the UDC in 1899, and the principal speaker at the event was Clement Evans. A smaller stone monument is also in the cemetery.

Gen. William Wofford (1824–84) is buried here. He opposed secession at the state convention but served with distinction in Virginia and commanded Thomas R. R. Cobb's famous legion after Cobb's death at Fredericksburg. On January 23, 1865, Gov. Joseph E. Brown recalled Wofford to raise seven hundred soldiers to feed the people and to quash the anarchy that had seized parts of northern Georgia since Sherman's forces had left the area.

During the skirmishing for Cassville, the Confederate line occupied this ridge. The Union line was to the north, and the city was caught in between. *East of U.S. 41 and south of the old courthouse square; the shell of the original depot remains at Cassville Station, to the southwest on the railroad along U.S. 41.*

Cartersville

On May 19–20, 1864, the Confederate rear guard barricaded the depot, knocking out blocks for firing ports. During the engagement, Sherman's forces burned the roof and floor. A large section of the original depot remains downtown, approximately 40 feet wide and 124 feet long. A Confederate monument stands on the courthouse grounds.

In the Bartow History Center (319 East Cherokee Avenue, P.O. Box 1239, Cartersville, GA 30120 [770] 382-3818), the Etowah Valley Historical Society maintains a museum with several Civil War exhibits.

Gen. Pierce M. B. Young (1836–96), who would have graduated in the West Point class of 1861, is buried in Oak Hill Cemetery. He had corresponded with every prominent Georgian asking whether he should resign his appointment or remain and receive his commission, and all had advised his departure. He served in Virginia with J. E. B. Stuart's cavalry while Federals occupied his Cartersville home, Walnut Grove.

William Weimann Mineral Museum. Featured here is a recreation of the nearby saltpeter cave and a display surrounded by photographs of mining operations. *Mineral Museum Drive, U.S. 441 and I-75, exit 126, P.O. Box 1255, Cartersville, GA 30120 (770) 386-0576.*

Etowah River Railroad Piers. These five stone piers supported the original Western and Atlantic Railroad bridge over the Etowah River. Confederates retreating from Cassville burned the bridge, and the new trestle was built downstream.

On the hill immediately to the north are Federal earthworks constructed to defend the railroad from Confederate raids. The bored garrison swam, hiked, played baseball, and hunted. A few were captured by Southerners. *Beside U.S. 41 at the Etowah River, three miles south of Cartersville.*

These lonely stone piers supported the Western and Atlantic Railroad bridge over the Etowah River during the Civil War.

Cooper's Furnace. The first iron foundries in Georgia were built here in the 1840s on Allatoona Creek. By the outbreak of the Civil War, Mark Cooper had established a rolling mill, a flour mill, and factories for weapons, tools, and utensils. These enterprises, which stretched for several miles and employed sixty people, flourished with the outbreak of the war. Georgia took control of the factories in 1863. On May 21, 1864, Federal cavalry burned the works before rejoining Sherman at Kingston. All that remains is this enormous stone blast furnace; other ruins are beneath Lake Allatoona. Cooper's yard engine, the *Yonah,* which was used to transfer goods to the Western and Atlantic Railroad, was standing on a siding here when the *General* thundered past. The locomotive was commandeered by William Fuller during his pursuit of Andrews's raiders. *At the end of River Road at Cooper's Furnace Day Use Area, two and one-half miles east of U.S. 41.*

The next road east leads to Allatoona Dam and a visitors center where the Army Corps of Engineers maintains a museum with displays of Civil War relics and materials related to Cooper's Furnace and the battle of Allatoona. *Allatoona Lake and Visitors Center, P.O. Box 487, Cartersville, GA 30120 (770) 382-4700.*

Allatoona

Retreating from Cassville, Johnston established heavily fortified positions in the rugged Allatoona Mountains. Sherman, realizing that his army could never break through these defenses, outflanked the Allatoona position by advancing to the southwest, hoping to reach Atlanta through Dallas. After Johnston abandoned Allatoona, Sherman left a strong garrison here to protect the Western and Atlantic Railroad and extensive storehouses. In October, when Hood attempted to draw Sherman out of Atlanta by driving north, part of his army assaulted the Union works at Allatoona. A desperate, hand-to-hand struggle ensued with heavy casualties on both sides. Because of Sherman's signaled promise of reinforcements, the Federal commander held his position despite severe losses. The Confederates were repulsed, and the heroic defense inspired the hymn, "Hold the Fort, for I Am Coming."

The village of Allatoona remains virtually unchanged since 1864. Beside the tracks is the grave of an unknown Confederate soldier, lovingly tended by railroad workers for more than a century. Surviving from the battle are two antebellum homes and a brick structure that was a store. On the lawn of the Clayton-Mooney House (1830) is a marker honoring twenty-one unknown soldiers

This house witnessed savage fighting at Allatoona and served as a hospital.

who were buried there after the battle. The house, which was a Union command post and a hospital for both sides, has blood-stains on the floor and bullet holes in the walls. During the war the railroad passed to the east of the buildings. Lake Allatoona covers the site of a blockhouse that Hood succeeded in capturing, and to the south is a hill where Confederate artillery supported the October attack.

The deep pass, excavated from rock, and the eastern redoubt remain, owned primarily by the corps of engineers. The Etowah Valley Historical Society is clearing trails, and the Georgia Civil War Commission hopes to purchase additional land, particularly the star fort on the western slope. Confederates attacked from the north and west above the Clayton House and the present Carterville-Emerson-Allatoona Road. Union warehouses were below the forts in the pass. *Allatoona is on GA 397 two miles east of U.S. 41.*

Emerson, called Stegall's Station when Johnston camped there on May 20, was renamed after the war for Governor Brown's middle name. *It is on U.S. 41 south of Cartersville.*

Acworth

Federals occupied the community in June 1864 and used churches as hospitals and homes as officers quarters. "We left the town in a heap of ruins," wrote one of Sherman's officers in November.

After a brief rest at Kingston, Sherman abruptly marched around Johnston's position at Allatoona, hoping to reach Dallas before the Confederates could respond. Confederate and Union cavalry clashed at Raccoon Creek Church on GA 113 during the shift to Dallas. On Taft Road in Stilesboro is the massive Stilesboro Academy (1859), which closed in 1861 when the students went to war. Sherman moved south from Kingston and Cartersville and crossed the Etowah River on pontoon bridges near Milam's Bridge at Euharlee, the bridge having been torched by retreating Confederate cavalry, at Gillem's Bridge (today Harden Bridge) on the Kingston-Euharlee Road (today Harden Bridge Road), and at Island Ford. The Union forces converged on Euharlee and Stilesboro. McPherson approached Dallas from the west, and Thomas and Schofield moved to the southeast, passing on May 23–24.

Schofield and Thomas traveled on parallel roads to Dallas: Schofield to the east via Sligh's Mill (where he camped a night) to Burnt Hickory (today Huntsville), and Thomas along the center to Burnt Hickory. McPherson swung west to Taylorsville, Aragon, Rockmart, and Van Wert to Yorkville, atop Dugdown Mountain, and then moved east to Dallas.

Paulding County

New Hope Church

Johnston immediately discovered Sherman's movement and shifted his armies west, blocking Sherman's advance with an impregnable ten-mile-long defensive line, resulting in two weeks of intense fighting.

When Union Gen. John Geary reached New Hope Church on May 25, four miles east of Dallas, he reported a heavy concentration of Confederates. Sherman refused to believe that the enemy had reacted so quickly and ordered an immediate attack. Repeated assaults were smashed by the concentrated fire of Southern infantry and artillery. New Hope Church came to be remembered by the Federals as the "Hell Hole."

New Hope Church State Historical Site. Behind the white frame church is a small state park honoring the soldiers of the Confederacy and containing the grave of an officer, Mississippi Lt. Col. John Herrod, who fell defending the position. Sections of Confederate trenches are still visible to the rear. The Confederate line stretched through the cemetery north of GA 381, with some Confederates fighting from behind the headstones. The original log New Hope Church occupied the site of the stone store. Much of the battlefield where the Federals fell is now being developed for a housing tract.

Across the road and behind the brick Baptist church is the final Atlanta campaign pavilion, a small monument containing a relief map and historical marker that describe the battles and stalemate here and Sherman's eventual flanking of Johnston's line. In front of the church is a WPA stone honoring both the Federal and the Confederate soldiers who fought at New Hope Church. *On GA 381 three miles east of Dallas.*

To the southwest of GA 341 between Dallas and New Hope Church is Ellsberry Mountain, part of the Confederate line. Johnston maintained an observation post on the peaks. His headquarters, just south of the church, was in the William Wigley Home, which no longer stands.

Roxana on GA 381 was the intersection of the Dallas-Acworth and Burnt Hickory Roads, which Hardee and Hood used on May 24 to get to the fight at New Hope Church and Dallas. McPherson marched through on June 5 en route to his outflanking the Confederate positions around Dallas.

Pickett's Mill

Sherman was stymied by the resolute Confederate resistance at New Hope Church. Unable to break through, he resumed the strategy of flanking movements in an attempt to turn Johnston's right. On May 27 he sent a division to Pickett's Mill with orders to rout the small Confederate contingent he expected to find guarding the area. Johnston had again anticipated Sherman, and Patrick Cleburne's division was waiting. Three uncoordinated Union attacks were broken at a terrible cost. Union casualties totaled 467 in the half-hour clash.

Pickett's Mill State Historic Site. The state has purchased the 765-acre battlefield and recently developed it into what many consider to be the best preserved Civil War battlefield in the country. There are miles of infantry trenches, earthworks that protected artillery batteries (including Hazen's Hill, with a four-gun position), home sites, and the remains of the mill itself. Three loop tours between one and two miles in length explain the wilderness battle. Prominent sites are the ridge occupied by the Confederates and the ravine where the Federals were decimated. The new visitors center has exhibits and a seventeen-minute video that describes the battle. *Pickett's Mill State Historic Site, 2640 Mount Tabor Road, Dallas, GA 30132 (770) 443-7850.*

Dallas

On May 28, 1864, expecting Sherman to shift troops from his right to his left to outflank the Confederates, Johnston attacked the Federal lines at Dallas, hoping to catch them as they withdrew. The Union troops, however, were still strongly entrenched, and in three futile attacks, the Orphan Brigade suffered 600 casualties to 380 Federals.

The Dallas battlefield, along Old U.S. 278, survived intact until the summer of 1995 when much of it was bulldozed and the soil trucked away as filler for a shopping center. The property was thought to contain the graves of three hundred Confederates and had earthworks. The site will be developed for commercial purposes or apartments. South of Dallas on the east side of Academy Road off Hardee Street was the grave of an unknown Confederate soldier, apparently killed at the nearby battle and now interred in the Morris family cemetery. Sherman's headquarters on the Dallas line was the Henderson House on East Memorial Drive.

Cobb County

Gilgal Church

The original church was destroyed in the battle fought here on June 15, 1864, but Sydney K. Kerksis purchased this land and reconstructed a portion of a typical Civil War earthwork in a small roadside park. The trench is six feet deep with the dirt piled into a protective wall toward the enemy. The inner trench face is reinforced with large logs, and a head log on top was used to protect the soldiers firing through the gaps beneath it. Timbers running from the front of the trench to the rear allowed any logs dislodged by artillery fire to skid harmlessly over the soldiers.

The Federals marched along the Kennesaw-Due West Road near the intersection with Acworth-Due West Road, passing prominent Lost Mountain to attack Johnston's Brushy Mountain line. Thomas made his headquarters at Mars Hill Church, just south of U.S. 41, and his army crossed Mascon Bridge over Allatoona Creek.

Confederates faced heavy artillery fire at Mud Creek on GA 120. They occupied the eastern ridge; the Federals were to the west. At the Darby House, west of the creek, Union batteries deployed and troops formed for battle.

Kennesaw Mountain

Both armies shifted east on June 10 when Sherman flanked Johnston out of the Dallas position. While Sherman spent several days regrouping, Johnston constructed a seventeen-mile defensive line north of Marietta. It was anchored on three mountains from east to west: Brushy, Pine, and Lost. Sherman slowly drove the Confederates from this thinly manned position only to find a second, infinitely stronger line behind it. Anchored on the twin peaks of Kennesaw Mountain, it extended several miles west over wooded ridges.

The rugged terrain combined with constant rains to make the countryside a quagmire, preventing Sherman from outflanking the Kennesaw line. Frustrated, on June 27 he ordered two assaults on the Confederate position. McPherson's attack at Pigeon Hill was easily defeated, and Thomas launched a determined strike on Cheatham Hill farther west that was repulsed at a high cost.

The armies remained stalemated at Kennesaw for another week, but the roads dried out and Schofield was able to move to a position behind Johnston. The Confederates retreated to establish two more defensive lines, at Smyrna and at the Chattahoochee River, but Sherman flanked each. On July 9 Johnston withdrew behind the Chattahoochee, just miles from Atlanta.

Kennesaw Mountain National Battlefield Park. This facility includes three major sites: the mountain itself, Cheatham Hill, and the Kolb Farm. The visitors center at the foot of Kennesaw Mountain offers beautiful views of the peaks where the Federals staged a feinting action. The center features uniforms and artifact displays, maps, drawings, and pictures that illustrate the fighting at Kennesaw. A fifteen-minute slide show further describes the movements in the Atlanta campaign. Sixteen miles of trails connect battlefield sites, passing a dozen miles of earthworks and crossing mountains, meadows,

Union artillery heavily shelled Confederate positions on Kennesaw Mountain.

forests, and streams. A park brochure and tour guide is available at the visitors center.

A steep road behind the center winds to the top of Kennesaw Mountain, past the inspiring Georgia Monument. On holidays and weekends, only park buses are allowed. An observation platform near the summit contains a monument to the Georgian generals who fought at Kennesaw. Artillery positions have been recreated along a steep path to the crest. These works had been leveled during spectacular cannon duels, but casualties were light. The guns were laboriously dragged up the steep peak by hand. Interesting markers point out the proximity of Atlanta to the south, the Allatoona Mountains to the north, Little Kennesaw to the west—held by William W. Loring, and the three peaks that constituted Johnston's first defensive line—Lost Mountain to the west, Pine Mountain to the north, and Brushy Mountain to the northeast—at the railroad tracks near U.S. 41. The views from Kennesaw are stunning. One can easily imagine that day in 1864 when the Confederates oversaw the awful specter of the battle below.

Cheatham Hill is one of the most impressive Civil War sites in Georgia. Along the roadway to Cheatham Hill are preserved sections of Confederate trenches and artillery batteries and a pink granite monument erected by the state of Texas in 1964 honoring her sons in the Army of Tennessee. Eight thousand Federals attacked across the open fields to the front.

From a large battery at the end of the road, which was instrumental in repulsing the assault, a path leads beside extensive earthworks to the "bloody angle," the primary objective of the failed Union attack. A display here depicts the scene as the assault peaked and shattered in hand-to-hand combat with bayonets and the Confederates throwing rocks and using their muskets as clubs.

The park originated in 1899 when the state of Illinois, which suffered the most losses in the fight, purchased this part of the battlefield. The impressive Illinois Monument honors 480 men who died at Cheatham Hill. The memorial, thirty-four feet square and twenty-five feet high, features a seven-foot-high bronze soldier clutching his rifle. It was dedicated on the fiftieth anniversary of the battle—June 27, 1914. Illinois donated the land to the War Department in 1917.

At the base of the hill is the Tunnel Monument, where Union soldiers burrowed beneath the Confederate lines and planned to explode a mine, just as Federal besiegers did at Vicksburg and Petersburg. Also here is the grave of an unknown soldier, discovered in 1934 by Civilian Conservation Corps (CCC) crews. Facing the monument is a gentle slope, the killing field, and a trail that follows the Union attack route. A monument honors Col. Dan McCook, Sherman's former law partner, who died trying to rally his troops. Notice here that trenches joining the main line of defense run in a different direction. This was a protection against enfilading fire that occurred at a salient when

The imposing Illinois monument honors the Union troops who fought at Cheatham Hill.

the enemy was on either side of the work and could bombard the length of the line. It also allowed for ammunition and reinforcements to be rushed safely to the front and for the wounded to be removed.

Trails from a parking area at Pigeon Hill lead to well-preserved earthworks at the foot of the ridge where McPherson's attack was soundly repulsed. There are several positions between Pigeon Hill and Cheatham Hill that were important during the Kennesaw Mountain campaign—notably, Horseshoe Bend and Bald Knob.

The last portion of the park is the Kolb Farm (1836) where, several days before the battle, Hood launched an impetuous and unauthorized assault against a strong Federal position. The determined Confederate attack was decimated by massed artillery fire. Union sharpshooters were positioned in the house and along the fences. The National Park Service has restored the log home, which was Federal Gen. Joseph Hooker's headquarters and suffered severe damage during the engagement, but it is not open to the public. Between the Kolb Farm and Cheatham Hill is the marked site from which Sherman watched the June 22 attack at the spot where Thomas's five brigades formed for their attack on Cheatham Hill.

On Gilbert Road, off Stilesboro Road west of the visitors center, is the undeveloped site of a twenty-four-gun Federal battery that pounded Confederate positions on Kennesaw Mountain.

In a rifle pit at the foot of Little Kennesaw, near a series of stone lunettes, Sgt. C. E. Dale of the Ninth Texas Infantry carved C.E. DALE IX TEX in Roman-style lettering. He was killed on October 5 at Allatoona. Farmers found the nearly inaccessible site in 1931. *Kennesaw Mountain National Battlefield Park is two miles north of Marietta off U.S. 41 on Old U.S. 41 at Stilesboro Road: 900 Kennesaw Mountain Drive, P.O. Box 1167, Marietta, GA 31044-4854 (770) 427-4686.*

Gen. Leonidas Polk Monument. A twenty-foot-high marble shaft on private property atop Pine Mountain marks the spot where Polk was killed by an artillery shell as he surveyed the Federal lines with Johnston and Hardee. It was placed in 1902 by a Marietta Confederate veteran and his wife. *Beaumont Road, on a short path from the historical marker.*

The Brushy Mountain line that extended west to Lost Mountain has been largely destroyed by construction work on I-75 and I-575 and development along the highways, but it is being studied with an eye to preserving a portion.

At the intersection of Burnt Hickory Road and Ernest Barrett Parkway in West Cobb is the Wallace House, headquarters of Oliver O. Howard, who founded the Freedmen's Bureau following the war and for whom Howard University is named. Southwest of Marietta on Powder Springs Road is the Cheney House, Schofield's headquarters, which Sherman visited several times. At the corner of Macland Road and Powder Springs Road near the Kolb Farm is the William G. MacAdoo House, the birthplace of Woodrow Wilson's treasury secretary in 1863. The home was used by Federal sharpshooters during the battle. Artillery Hill, north of Kennesaw Mountain, saw sharp fighting and contains a prominent cannon emplacement. John Geary's division suffered five hundred casualties at Pine Knob on June 1 as Hooker advanced on the Kennesaw-Due West Road. Fifty acres of the battlefield remain, containing well-preserved earthworks. Parts of these sites may be preserved.

Kennesaw

Known during the war as Big Shanty (shanties were used to house railroad workers), Kennesaw was the starting point of the Great Locomotive Chase. A team of union saboteurs, led by James J. Andrews, boarded a train drawn by the engine *General* in Marietta on April 12, 1862. When the passengers and crew disembarked for breakfast at Kennesaw, the Federals stole the train, intending to destroy sixteen railroad bridges between Kennesaw and Chattanooga as an aid to Northern forces intent on capturing the latter. The *General*'s heroic engineer, William Fuller, chased his engine for eight hours and eighty-seven miles by foot, on polecar, and by commandeering three locomotives encountered along the way, having to run two in reverse since there were no roundhouses in the vicinity. The raiders were caught near Ringgold and imprisoned. Eight were executed and the rest escaped or were paroled. All save Andrews, a civilian, earned the newly created Congressional Medal of Honor.

Kennesaw served as Sherman's headquarters during the Kennesaw Mountain fighting. Following a fierce fight in October 1864, Confederate forces captured a Federal garrison quartered in the old Lacy Hotel, which Sherman later burned in November. Kennesaw was also the site of Camp McDonald, established by Governor Brown in June 1861, the largest training facility for Southern recruits in the state.

The *General* came under artillery fire when it brought ammunition to Johnston on June 27, 1864, at Kennesaw. On September 1 it was laboring south on the Macon Railroad with Hood's munitions when Sherman cut the road at Rough and Ready (Mountain View), forcing the train to return in reverse to Atlanta. The locomotive survived the destruction of five engines and eighty-one cars when Hood evacuated the city, but it was nearly scrapped after the war. The engine was restored but suffered two wrecks near Kingston. It was featured at several Civil War reunions until it seemed to just disappear. Later, the *General* was found on a siding near Vinings, restored again, and displayed at many fairs. It ran the route of the chase in 1962 for the centennial of the war and appeared in 120 cities. Georgia and Chattanooga battled for years over possession of the locomotive, but federal courts returned the engine in 1972 to Kennesaw.

The celebrated locomotive General *is pictured from its working days, before it came to be housed in the Big Shanty Museum.*

Big Shanty Museum. The *General* is permanently housed in a converted cotton gin, impressively displayed on rails at a recreated station along with other Civil War and railroad exhibits. A wonderful series of stained glass depicts the *General*'s adventures in an auditorium where a slide show is presented. Across the tracks from the museum, in Commemorative Park, are a stone monument marking the start of the chase (a similar one signifies the end of the chase near Ringgold) and a plaque honoring Fuller's determined recapture of his engine. Each April Kennesaw hosts a Big Shanty Festival to celebrate the Great Locomotive Chase. *2829 Cherokee Street (Old 41), Kennesaw, GA 30144 (770) 427-2117; (800) 742-6897.*

Those members of Andrews's raiders who were executed following the affair are buried in the Chattanooga National Cemetery, at Holtzclaw and Bailey. Their graves are clustered around a stone monument topped by a bronze replica of the *General.*

A walking tour guide to Kennesaw is available at the museum. It highlights the site of the Lacy Hotel, a little south of the present depot, the Big Shanty Restaurant (which now has a policy of not allowing locomotives to be parked outside unattended), and the site of Camp McDonald, between North Main and Dallas. The camp was established here because of the presence of a large spring, which is preserved in a park behind the Kennesaw Municipal Building. Many reunions of Confederate veterans have been held here.

Marietta

Marietta Confederate Cemetery. This plot, part of the city cemetery, was set aside by Jane Glover, Ann Moyer, other residents, and the city for the soldiers who were killed in a train wreck in 1863. Men who died in area hospitals were buried here (five hundred in July 1864 during fighting at Kennesaw). In 1866 the state funded a program to gather the bodies of the men who died at Chickamauga and on battlefields of the Atlanta campaign for interment. The plan was administered by Mary J. Green of Resaca and Mrs. Charles Williams of the Ladies Memorial Association. The original wooden grave markers were replaced in 1902 with marble gravestones, but most of the three thousand headstones are blank. Monuments list how many soldiers there are from each state. Tennessee has the most (325); Georgia is fourth, behind Alabama and Mississippi, but many Georgians were reburied in hometowns. The first burial here was a doctor, and the last, in 1989, was a soldier uncovered by construction activity. Most men who died in a local Confederate home were buried here; the last survivor was a black servant of a Confederate officer.

A twenty-five-foot-tall shaft honoring these men and Cobb County's Confederate veterans is near a gazebo. Clement A. Evans gave the principal speech on July 7, 1908, when the entire Georgia General Assembly adjourned early to attend. The 6-pounder bronze cannon on display was one of two used by cadets of the Georgia Military Institute during Sherman's march across the state. Captured at Savannah by Union forces, the cannon was returned in 1910.

Part of Citizen's Cemetery is at the corner of North 120 Loop and Cemetery Street, at Powder Springs Road. Gen. William Phillips (1824–1908) is buried here. He fought in western Virginia, lost an eye, contracted typhoid, and was discharged only to find his home and factories destroyed by Sherman.

A brochure guide to the Confederate cemetery is available at the Marietta Welcome Center in the old depot, which also offers a wonderful driving tour to Civil War sites in the city, *The Cannonball Trail,* and a walking tour of historic Marietta. *No. 4 Depot Street, Marietta, GA 30060 (770) 429-1115.*

Marietta National Cemetery. Established in 1866, this cemetery is the resting place for 10,132 (3,000 unidentified) Federal soldiers who fell south of Resaca during the Atlanta campaign. The donor of the land, Unionist Henry Greene Cole, hoped that soldiers of both armies would be buried here as a symbol of reconciliation, but the proposal was rejected. For many years former slaves from the Atlanta area met here on Memorial Day to celebrate their emancipation. Ceremonies to honor the slain are held annually on Memorial Day on the beautifully landscaped grounds. Monuments have been erected by several states in memory of sons buried here, the fallen of Resaca, Adairsville, Cassville, Dallas, New Hope Church, Pickett's Mill, Kennesaw Mountain, and the Atlanta battles. Both the Confederate and national cemeteries have good views of Kennesaw Mountain, near which many of the men died.

Mountainous north Georgia was the sanctuary of draft evaders, Unionist guerrillas, and thieving raiders. The Home Guard and Georgia Militia fought them in a cruel personal war; executions and persecutions of entire families were common. With Union Gen. George Thomas's permission, James G. Brown in 1864 sought to recruit a Federal unit from these hills, but he netted only three hundred.

On November 5, 1864, Col. James Findley of the First Georgia State Cavalry captured twenty-one Unionists at Bucktown in Gilmer County. Four were killed in the skirmish, additional sympathizers were arrested in Dawsonville, and twelve deserters were executed on November 7 in Gainesville. In July 1887 they were moved to this cemetery—Section E, Graves 6,012–6,023. *550 Washington Street, Northeast, several blocks east of the business district, Marietta, GA 30060 (770) 428-5631.*

The Kennesaw House (1855) was a resort hotel called the Fletcher House where James Andrews and his raiders spent the night before seizing the *General.* Confederate casualties were treated here until the summer of 1864. Sherman established his headquarters in the hotel on July 3, then partially burned it in November at the start of his March to the Sea. *Beside the welcome center in the depot, at the corner of Depot Street and Whitlock.*

Georgia Military Institute (1851). Two hundred cadets from the institute, aged fifteen to eighteen, joined the Georgia Militia for the latter stages of the Atlanta campaign and the March to the Sea. Earlier they

had helped drill recruits at Camp McDonald. Seventeen campus buildings were used as a large hospital by both armies. Sherman ordered
them burned in November 1864. He spared the home of the founder,
Col. Arnoldus Brumby (472 Powder Springs Road, 1854), which
remains. For decades the grounds were the Marietta Country Club, a
hilltop site with good views of Kennesaw, Lost, and Pine Mountains,
but a ritzy complex will soon occupy the site. GMI's second bronze
howitzer, displayed for years at the country club, will be positioned at
the entrance. *Opposite the city cemetery on Powder Springs Road.*

The First Presbyterian Church (189 Church Street, 1852), utilized as a
hospital by both sides, was so damaged that the U.S. government paid
a three-thousand-dollar repair bill. Federals also used Saint James Episcopal Church (148 Church Street) next door. It burned in 1964, but an
original chapel contains the organ that Union soldiers filled with
molasses. Fair Oaks (505 Kennesaw Avenue, 1850) was Johnston's
headquarters for the Kennesaw campaign, and Gen. William Loring
was at Oakton (581 Kennesaw Avenue, 1838). The Archibald Howell
House (303 Kennesaw Avenue, 1848) was occupied during the war's
last months by Union Gen. Henry M. Judah, who accepted the Confederate surrender at Kingston and provided food for local residents.
Andrew J. Hansell, a state militia colonel and aide to Governor Brown,
lived at Tranquilla (435 Kennesaw Avenue, 1849). Mrs. Hansell refused
to vacate when Union officers arrived and so she shared her home with
the occupiers. When the Bostwick-Fraser House (325 Atlanta Street,
1844) was a Union hospital, Fanny Fraser served as a nurse.

Sherman fortified the courthouse, which was east of the present
one, and nearby houses. Federals burned the courthouse and much
of the town, particularly around the public square, in November
1864. Confederate troops drilled on the square, which now features
a children's playhouse replica of the *General.*

The 1848 House (780 Cobb Drive-GA 280), a restaurant on the
National Register, was the center of a three-thousand-acre plantation that was the site of a rear-guard clash on July 3. It was used as
a Union hospital and quarters until after the battle of Allatoona Pass
in October, when it was stripped of valuables. Bullets found on the
grounds are displayed, and one is embedded in an inner door. The
Planter's Restaurant (129 Garrison Drive, 1848) was the Glover
House, which also witnessed skirmishes on July 3.

Episcopal Cemetery. Noted Civil War artist Alfred R. Waud is buried here. *Winn Street between Polk and Whitlock.*

Concord

Ruff's Gristmill (1850s) on Nickajack Creek was the site of a battle, one of several that erupted as Sherman moved south from Kennesaw Mountain toward Johnston's river line. Martin Ruff's house, an emergency hospital during the battle, and the Gann House (1853), where the family was forced to quarter fifteen Union officers for a period, also survive. Both are on the National Register. Although a woolen mill that manufactured Confederate uniforms and a sawmill were destroyed, the gristmill was spared for its food production use. The mills were rebuilt, and lumber from the sawmill was used to rebuild the Western and Atlantic Railroad. The ruins of the woolen mill remain. The historic covered bridge (1872) replaces one believed destroyed during the war. *At Concord Covered Bridge on Concord Bridge Road, between Smyrna and Marietta.*

The River Line

To slow Sherman's pursuit between Marietta and the Chattahoochee River, Johnston directed Francis A. Shoup to construct a line that stretched for four miles and was one mile in depth. It consisted of forty unique blockhouses (called shoupades) with overlapping fields of fire. They were placed eighty yards apart and defended by eighty men. The double log walls—with earth fill—were twelve feet thick. Between each position was a two-cannon redan, the whole connected by deep trenches and log stockades eight feet high. Heavier fortifications contained 20-pounder Parrott rifles removed from Mobile's seacoast defenses, and at each end of the line were large artillery forts. One of these, a seven-gun battery at the mouth of Nickajack Creek, is being preserved as a park.

Vining's Mountain

From this 1,170-foot height Sherman first looked down on Atlanta. Union batteries dueled with the Confederates across the river, and during the siege a railroad depot established here supplied the Federals and evacuated casualties. From here on July 14 Sherman issued Special Field Order No. 35, outlining his plan to broach the

Chattahoochee River. When he abandoned the siege lines and swung southwest to sever the railroads, Sherman heavily fortified this site.

The original home (1839) of founder Hardy Pace was occupied by Sherman for eleven days but destroyed after its use as a Union hospital. The Paces fled to Milledgeville, where Pace died. His widow returned with his body and in 1866 joined three former slave cabins under one roof to form a new home, which remains (268 Paces Mill Road). A nearby spring spa called Pavilion House was constructed by Governor Brown. Unfortunately, Vining's Mountain is succumbing rapidly to commercial development. *North of the Chattahoochee River on West Paces Ferry Road.*

At nearby Bolton, on GA 3-Old U.S. 41, Johnston crossed the Chattahoochee. A Confederate wagon train barely escaped capture by Union cavalry, but when the pontoon bridge was cut loose, it swung to the Union side and was captured. On July 17 Thomas crossed the Chattahoochee at Pace's Ferry, just south of Vinings at the Lovett School, and Power's Ferry, then marched south on Howell Mill Road and Northside Drive. Schofield crossed at Sope Creek, between Power's and Johnson's Ferries, and advanced toward Buckhead.

Fulton County

Sope Creek Ruins

The Marietta Paper Mill is rumored to have produced paper for Confederate currency. The mill is close to where Sherman first forced passage across the Chattahoochee. Schofield's men waded across on July 7, forcing Johnston to abandon the river line. Kenner Garrard's Federal cavalry had destroyed the factory several days earlier. The mill operated until 1902, burning several times. The extensive stone ruins are just below the bridge on Paper Mill Road, between Marietta and Sandy Springs, and are part of the Chattahoochee River National Recreation Area. Follow the paths beside the creek; ruins can be found on both banks.

Roswell

Johnston's river line on the north bank of the Chattahoochee brought the Federals temporarily to bay. To outflank the position, Sherman shifted his cavalry and McPherson's army east to the industrial center of Roswell, where his crossing forced the Confederates to withdraw to Atlanta's outer defenses.

As Union troops approached, the owners of the clothing mills in the area, the King family, fled, allegedly with their gold. Locals then raided the King mansions, stores, and mills. Temporary ownership was transferred to Theophilus Roche, an employee of only one year, with the hope that his ability to claim foreign ownership might save the mills. Roche raised the French flag above the Ivy Mill, but Garrard's men found "CSA" woven into the cloth being made. Sherman ordered the mills burned and the employees arrested. They were charged with treason and sent north of the Ohio River by way of Marietta, where they met other workers from Sweetwater Creek. Under guard July 6–10, they were loaded into boxcars and taken to Northern prisons. Some died of typhoid, others took the oath of allegiance and were released, and some later returned to Georgia. Roche also rode the rails. This was one of the great atrocities committed in Georgia, a barbarous act condemned by both sides.

Roswell is a beautifully preserved antebellum town with many historic homes that were spared by the Federals. Of particular Civil War interest is Roswell Presbyterian Church (755 Mimosa Avenue, 1840). Used as a Federal hospital, this building contains a small museum that preserves several unique artifacts from the war, including a checkerboard carved by Union soldiers on a cabinet door and a silver communion service hidden during the Union occupation by Miss Fannie Whitemore to prevent its theft. Great Oaks (786 Mimosa Boulevard, 1842) was headquarters for Garrard's cavalry. Allenbrook (227 Atlanta Street, 1840) was the home and office of Roche. Naylor Hall (Canton Street near Goulding Place, 1840) was heavily damaged. Mimosa Hall (127 Bulloch Avenue, 1847) was purchased after the war by Col. Andrew J. Hansell of Marietta.

Bulloch Hall (1840). This beautiful Greek Revival structure, owned by the city of Roswell, has several artifacts from the Union occupation when it was used as a Federal barracks. In 1853 Teddy Roosevelt's parents had been married here. *180 Bulloch Avenue, P.O. Box 1309, Roswell, GA 30077 (770) 992-1731.*

Several original mill buildings, some dating to 1839, remain today. On Sloan Street are The Bricks, some of the first apartments in

These brick apartments, some of the first in the country, housed Union casualties in Roswell.

America, built for mill workers and used by the Federals as hospitals. Nearby, at the end of Mill Street, is a large parking area from which stairs lead to Vickery Creek Gorge, where Union cavalry had orders to burn the machine house. The brick shell and the dam that provided water for turning the machinery can be seen. On the highway above the existing mill-shopping complex is the Public House Restaurant, which was the company store. Garrard destroyed everything else, including a four-story cotton mill.

The highway bridge across the Chattahoochee on U.S. 19 marks the site of a covered bridge that retreating Confederates burned as Garrard approached. In just sixty hours houses and mill buildings were dismantled by the Federals to build a twin-span bridge 710 feet long, 18 feet wide, and 14 feet high. When McPherson's Army of the Tennessee crossed on July 10 during a tremendous thunderstorm, a dozen men were killed, trees were split, and muskets were discharged by the lightning. McPherson swung east to Decatur to cut the Augusta Railroad.

Roswell is on the Chattahoochee River, north of Atlanta on U.S. 19. The Roswell Historical Society has an outstanding guide to the city. *227 Atlanta Street, Roswell, GA 30075 (770) 992-1665.*

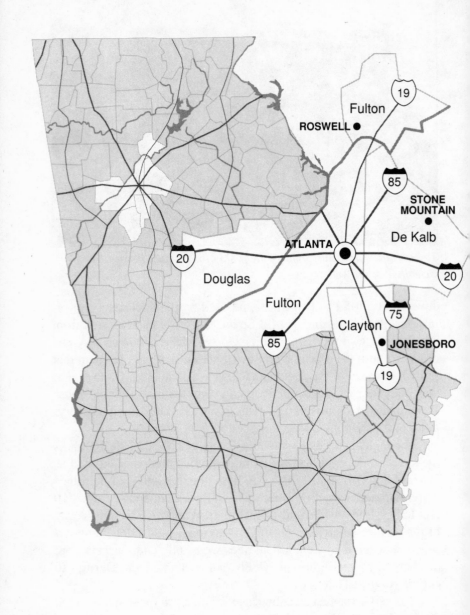

⊰3⊱
Metropolitan Atlanta

B Y 1864 ATLANTA was the second most important city in the Confederacy. Its location in the Deep South made it relatively safe for the industrial production of war goods, and factories had been relocated here from every part of the shrinking nation. Cannon, rifles, pistols, shells, cartridges, wagons, uniforms, swords, shoes, steel plate for ironclads, and innumerable items were being manufactured in large quantities. The four railroads that met in Atlanta carried this production throughout the Confederacy to enable the armies to continue fighting, and the great agricultural bounty of the Deep South and the Trans-Mississippi region was funneled through Atlanta to feed several hundred thousand soldiers. As the fighting neared Georgia, vast numbers of wounded and ill soldiers received care in the great hospital complexes of the city. All of this also made Atlanta the second most important target in the Confederacy.

After four major battles and two months of siege and bombardment, which resulted in thirty-five thousand Confederate casualties, Sherman captured Atlanta on September 2, 1864. Eleven weeks later the Federals abandoned the city and began the March to the Sea. Every railroad facility, factory, warehouse, and foundry was demolished. Atlanta was torched; only four hundred of fifteen hundred structures survived. A survey of the area for Gov. Joseph E. Brown reported that thirty-two hundred homes had been burned in the city and another eighteen hundred in the immediate area. The fall of Atlanta revived Northern morale and was a significant factor in the reelection of Abraham Lincoln, who continued the war to its victorious conclusion five months later.

Atlanta History Center

Featured in a new facility are five exhibits concerning the history of Atlanta, including one dealing exclusively with the Atlanta campaign and the Civil War in Georgia. Each July, on or about the anniversary date of the battle of Atlanta, the center hosts a Civil War encampment with reenactors demonstrating camp life: drilling, cooking, diversions, music, weapons handling, and so forth. *130 West Paces Ferry Road Northwest, Atlanta, GA 30305-1366 (404) 814-4000.*

Peachtree Creek

Sherman bridged the Chattahoochee at several points, forcing Johnston to withdraw to a position just north of Atlanta, along Peachtree Creek. When Sherman's largest force, Thomas's Army of the Cumberland, crossed the creek, Johnston intended to strike and destroy it. On the eve of battle, however, Confederate Pres. Jefferson Davis relieved Johnston and replaced him with John B. Hood. Hood immediately followed the same plan, but his assault was delayed, giving Thomas time to entrench. The Confederate attack was launched piecemeal, resulting in terrible losses.

A large stone monument, dedicated in 1944 by the Atlanta Historical Society to honor the Federals and the Confederates who fought here, is on the grounds of Piedmont Hospital on U.S. 19 (Peachtree Street at Brighton Road). Near it is a plaque set in stone marking the spot where the battle began.

Just off U.S. 19 on Collier Road is Tanyard Creek Park, in the area where the heaviest fighting occurred. It was created by the city of Atlanta during the centennial celebration of the battle in 1964. Nine large descriptive plaques were set on cement stands, but three are now missing. Across the road are the millstones and pieces of machinery from Collier's Mill, a battlefield landmark and casualty. The mill's foundation can be seen in the creek.

In a small park at Peachtree Battle Avenue and Peachtree Road is a memorial to Confederate soldiers dedicated by the Old Guard of Georgia. Another stone monument is at Peachtree and Palisades Road. A small stone with a plaque notes the position of Howell's

Millstones and machinery mark the site of Collier's Mill, a landmark during the battle of Peachtree Creek.

Georgia Battery from which Capt. Evan Howell fired on the Federals occupying his grandfather's plantation.

The battle area was centered around Howell Mill Road, Northside Drive, Collier Road, Peachtree Battle Avenue, and Peachtree Road. From the hill at the entrance to the Bitsy Grant Tennis Center, the battlefield can be seen to the east, from where Confederates left their works, which is marked by a stone at the intersection of Peachtree and Spring Streets.

The Confederates attacked north through Tanyard Creek Park, their battle line extending through the area of Piedmont Hospital north of Collier and up Northside Drive west of the park. Confederate Gen. C. H. Stevens was killed at the intersection of Twenty-eighth Street and Wycliff. At Collier's Mill the Federals, including future Pres. Benjamin Harrison, concentrated several artillery batteries that halted the Confederate drive.

Battle of Atlanta

After the repulse at Peachtree Creek, Hood withdrew to Atlanta's inner defenses and immediately prepared to launch an attack on

McPherson's Army of the Tennessee, which was closing on the city from Decatur after cutting Atlanta's railroad link with the Carolinas and Virginia. The engagement, remembered as the battle of Atlanta, was the costliest action of the campaign. A fierce Confederate assault ruptured the Federal line and threatened to roll up the Army of the Tennessee, but the gap was closed and successive Confederate attacks were destroyed by massed Federal artillery. Hood was forced to withdraw inside Atlanta's defenses.

The site of the battle has been covered by Atlanta's explosive growth, but two monuments remain. At the intersection of Glenwood Avenue and Wilkinson at I-20 is a cannon mounted on a concrete base. Here Federal pickets killed Confederate Gen. William T. Walker as the battle began. Nearby, at the intersection of Monument and McPherson, just off Glenwood, is a similar monument marking the place where James B. McPherson died when he inadvertently rode into a Confederate advance.

To launch his flank attack, Confederate Gen. William J. Hardee marched through the night on Peachtree Street to Five Points and down Capital Avenue almost to the Yellow River, being joined by Patrick Cleburne at Memorial. Hardee then turned up Bouldercrest to split his forces on Flat Shoals and Fayetteville Road. Confederate assaults were launched all along the Federal line, just north of Glenwood and farther north up Moreland where it intersects with DeKalb, which is the focal point of the Cyclorama display. The Confederate breakthrough occurred at Moreland and the Georgia Railroad, site of the contested DeGress Battery and Troup Hurt House and current site of the old East Atlanta Primitive Baptist Church on DeGress Avenue. Sherman's headquarters at the Augustus Hurt House, where McPherson's body had been carried, was on the grounds of the Carter Presidential Library on Copenhill Avenue Northeast. Leggett's Hill, the scene of desperate fighting, is at the I-20 exchange on Moreland.

Cyclorama and Grant Park. The Atlanta battlefield may have been lost to urban expansion, but the great conflict can be fully appreciated at the famous Cyclorama. It started in 1885 as a massive circular painting weighing eighteen thousand pounds. With a circumference of 385 feet and a height of 42 feet, it is the world's largest canvas. The work was commissioned by Union Gen. John A. Logan during an unsuccessful bid for the vice presidency. German artists from Milwaukee labored for two years to create it, constructing a forty-foot-high tower to examine the terrain of the battlefield and poring over veterans' reports of the struggle. The painting toured America until 1892 when it became a permanent landmark in Atlanta through the largess of philanthropist George V. Green. By 1926 it belonged to the city and was placed in its present structure. The diorama—a foreground of hills, ravines, cannon, wagons, rails, and fighting men (including a dead Clark Gable figure)—was added during the 1930s and blends perfectly with the painting to create a three-dimensional effect. A 182-seat theater slowly rotates while a light-and-sound show describes the battle of Atlanta as depicted on the canvas. It is a thrilling experience.

In another theater visitors view a film explaining the campaign that led to the battle. In the lobby is a cannon and the locomotive *Texas,* the last engine commandeered by the *General*'s conductor, William Fuller, during the famous chase. To prevent the scrapping of the *Texas* in 1907, the mayor of Atlanta, Courtland S. Winn, purchased it for the city. The locomotive was first displayed on rails at Fort Walker, but in 1936 it was restored and moved to the Cyclorama's basement.

A Civil War museum on the second floor of the Cyclorama features Civil War artifacts, large photographs of the generals who participated in the Atlanta campaign, a computer that reports the action on any given day of the war, and an exhibit highlighting the contributions of minorities to the war effort.

At the southwestern corner of the park is Fort Walker, a massive earthwork named for the Confederate general who died in the battle. It was part of an extensive system of defensive works that faced Sherman during the siege, when Atlanta was one of the most heavily fortified cities in the Confederacy. Ten miles of earthworks, studded with powerful artillery forts, ringed Atlanta at a distance of a mile and one-half from the center of town. The fortifications were designed by Col. Lemuel P. Grant, a native of Maine who in 1887 donated this land for the park that bears his name. The earthworks, fronted by log palisades and entanglements, were so formidable that

Sherman refused to attack the city. Most traces of the works have been covered in the course of Atlanta's growth.

The area of Atlanta University was the westernmost point of the city's fortifications. The intersection of Ashby and Fair was the site of Whitehall Fort, a major defensive position. Other forts were on the sites of Georgia Tech and the Georgian Terrace Hotel. WSB-TV (1601 West Peachtree Street) occupies a spot that was also on the outer works. A small stone marker in front of Peachtree Christian Church (1580 Peachtree Street) marks the Confederate outer defensive line on July 18. The Grant Mansion (1858), one of fifteen antebellum structures surviving in Atlanta, is crumbling nearby. The main entrance to Grant Park is at the intersection of Cherokee and Georgia. *800 Cherokee Avenue, Southeast, Atlanta, GA 30315 (404) 658-7625.*

Oakland Cemetery

Twenty-four hundred Confederates and twenty Federals are buried in the Confederate section. They died of wounds and disease in a complex of forty hospital buildings established at the fairgrounds or in the intense fighting during the battles for Atlanta. More than sixty thousand soldiers were treated locally. The graves were originally marked by wooden headboards, but in 1890 they were replaced with standard U.S. government round marble stones, although some pointed ones were added in 1951. A sixty-five-foot-tall obelisk of Stone Mountain granite pays homage to the fallen. Dedicated on Confederate Memorial Day 1874, when Gov. John B. Gordon spoke, it was then Atlanta's tallest structure. The base had been set four years earlier, October 15, 1870, the day of Robert E. Lee's funeral. Among the libations Masons poured on it was a bottle of champagne given by a Southern lady to an officer in 1862 to be opened when the Confederacy was independent. A monument to the Real Daughters of the Confederacy is in this section (real daughters are those whose fathers served in the Confederate armed forces; it would not include those whose grandfathers or other relatives were in uniform for the South). A number of civilians killed during Sherman's siege of the city are also buried at Oakland.

Beside the Confederate cemetery is the famed Lion sculpture, one of the most moving monuments in the nation. An imitation of the statue in Lucerne, Switzerland (dedicated in 1792 to sixteen faithful Swiss Guards who died protecting Marie Antoinette during the French Revolution), it depicts a grieving lion clutching a Confederate flag. The six-foot-high statue, carved from a fifteen-ton piece of Tate, Georgia, marble by T. M. Brady, was unveiled in April 1895. It honors the memory of several hundred unidentified Confederate soldiers buried in this plot and several thousand dead from the Atlanta battlefields who were reinterred at that time. Ceremonies commemorating the Southern dead have been held at Oakland since 1866.

Three Confederate generals are buried near the Lion in Block K: John B. Gordon, Clement A. Evans, and Alfred Iverson Jr. Gordon (1832–1904), a delegate to both the Alabama and Georgia state secession conventions, raised the Raccoon Roughs in northern Alabama and Georgia. Fighting in every eastern battle, he was wounded five times at Antietam and nursed to health by his wife, who accompanied him throughout the war. Gordon headed the largest brigade in the Confederate army, then commanded a division, led a corps, and by Appomattox had risen to lead half the army. It was Gordon, not Lee, who led the Confederates to stack their weapons at the surrender, when he instructed the men to return home and rebuild their lives. He was later governor of Georgia and served three terms in the U.S. Senate. Evans (1833–1911) was wounded five times, spent thirty years as a minister, and became a noted Confederate historian. Cavalry leader Alfred Iverson Jr. (1829–1911) served in Virginia, then defeated Sherman's troopers during Atlanta campaign raids at Sunshine Church, near his home. He had grown up in Washington, D.C., where his father served as a senator from Georgia.

In family plots are the graves of Georgia's wartime governor, Joseph Brown, and Confederate Gens. Lucius J. Gartrell, William S. Walker, Henry K. McCay, and Isaac W. Avery. Gartrell (1821–91) caught Francis S. Bartow as he fell at Manassas, where he also lost his sixteen-year-old son, Henry Clay Gartrell. Walker (1822–99) was captured in 1864 after riding into the Union lines. McCay (1820–86) was a teacher from Pennsylvania who commanded the Georgia Militia at Atlanta, Griswoldville, and Doctortown. Avery (1837–97) fought at Chickamauga and was wounded at New Hope Church.

Confederate Vice Pres. Alexander Stephens was interred in an Oakland vault from 1883 to 1884. Abraham Lincoln's brother-in-law, Benjamin H. Helm, a Confederate officer, suffered a mortal wound at Chickamauga and was temporarily buried here before being relocated in 1884 to a family plot in Elizabethtown, Kentucky. His funeral had been held at Saint Phillip's Episcopal Church.

Also buried in Oakland are the three men who lost and heroically recaptured the *General:* William Fuller, Jeff Cain, and Anthony Murphy. Ironically, Andrews's raiders also have a history in Oakland. On the inner brick wall facing Memorial Drive is a bronze plaque honoring seven raiders who were executed outside the wall and buried here, along with Andrews, who was executed nearby at the intersection of Juniper and Third. Their bodies were reinterred in the Chattanooga National Cemetery in 1887 at a ceremony attended by ten thousand people, including Fuller. The Ohio legislature placed a bronze replica of the *General* on a marble base among their graves. The raiders had been held in the Fulton County Jail, and eight escaped.

The fifteen-year-old fireman of the *Texas,* Henry Haney, became a high-ranking Atlanta fire chief. He died on November 19, 1923, outliving the last raider by one month, and is buried in Atlanta's Crestlawn Cemetery.

The grounds of Oakland Cemetery provide a grand view of Atlanta. A historical marker stands on the site of Mayor James E. Williams's home, from where Hood watched the battle of Atlanta. *248 Oakland Avenue Southeast, Atlanta, GA 30312 (404) 658-6019; (404) 688-2107.*

Beside the railroad tracks near the cemetery, at the Fulton Bag and Cotton Mill, was a rolling mill that supplied armor for Confederate ironclads. This was the place where Hood destroyed eighty-one boxcars and five locomotives loaded with ammunition when he abandoned the city. The resulting explosion was heard, felt, and seen for twenty miles.

Ezra Church

After the battle of Atlanta, Sherman had severed two of four railroads that supplied the city. His next move was to the southwest to cut the West Point and Macon Railroads. On July 28 Hood sent part of his force to stop the Federals near Ezra Church, but the Confederates were again committed piecemeal against a prepared adversary. Hood's losses were heavy, but the railroads were temporarily saved from destruction.

The battle site is in Mozley Park on Martin Luther King Jr. Drive, but only historical markers stand to describe the action. Inside the MLK entrance to Westview Cemetery, in Section 38, is a monument to the battle, a plaque surrounded by a brick wall. The old gatehouse at the Ralph David Abernathy Boulevard entrance marks the site of a Confederate almshouse, where refugees from the fighting in Tennessee and northern Georgia were housed. The monument atop the nearby hill in the cemetery was placed by Fulton County Confederates in memory of their comrades, one hundred of whom were interred around the statue, including veterans of this battle. There are two mortars in front of the monument, which stands on the site of a fifteen-gun battery. At the eastern edge of the outer cemetery drive is a single Confederate grave, that of Lt. Edward Clingman, who died in the battle. Behind the grave is a section of trench used first by Southern troops, then by Federals as they laid siege to Atlanta. Confederates marched to Ezra Church along Abernathy (Lickskillet Road).

Georgia offered plots in Westview in 1889 to Varina Davis following the death of her husband, Jefferson Davis, but the former president of the Confederacy was buried in New Orleans. In 1893 Varina decided that his final resting place should be in Richmond. Davis's remains were honored in 1893 as the funeral train passed through Georgia.

Buried here is Joel Chandler Harris, a noted author who witnessed Sherman's March to the Sea as a boy in Putnam County. *Westview Cemetery, 1680 Abernathy Boulevard, Atlanta, GA 30310 (404) 755-6611.*

Utoy Creek

Growing impatient with the siege, on August 8 Sherman directed assaults at Confederate positions protecting the railroad at Utoy Creek. They were beaten off with heavy Union losses.

Utoy Church (1828) was used as a Confederate hospital during the battle. At the northwestern corner of the adjacent cemetery are eighteen graves, the only fatalities the Southerners suffered in the battle. Beside the graves is a portion of Confederate trenches. *At Venetian and Cahaba in southwest Atlanta.*

The battle was fought to the west in Cascade Springs Nature Preserve, which is not open. The Confederate line was south of Cascade (the old Sandtown Road), on both sides of Willis Mill Road. Beside a historical marker on a golf course in Adams Park to the east is a shallow ditch that was a Confederate work.

Georgia State Capitol

The grounds of the capitol (1883) contain an impressive bronze equestrian statue of John B. Gordon, created in 1907 by Solon Borglum, the brother of the man who created Mount Rushmore and abandoned the work at Stone Mountain. Gordon was the first governor to serve in this capitol. The general sits astride his horse Marye, captured in battle at Chancellorsville in May 1863. There is a statue of Gov. Joseph E. Brown, also a U.S. senator and Georgia supreme court justice, and his wife. Several large bronze tablets erected by the UDC describe the fight for the city and Atlanta's surrender.

The equestrian statue of John B. Gordon, a prominent Confederate general on the Virginia battle front, was erected on the state capitol grounds.

On the first floor of the capitol, in the Georgia State Museum of Science and

The statue of Gov. Joseph E. Brown and his wife. The governor gave as much grief to Jefferson Davis as he did to Abraham Lincoln.

Industry, numerous Confederate flags belonging to Georgia regiments that fought in every theater of the war are mounted on the walls. Several of the tattered standards were surrendered at Appomattox and later returned, and many were torn in battle by shot. The flags are inscribed with the name of the unit to which they belonged. As the war progressed the men added the names of battles in which they had seen action. On the main floor are busts and portraits of several Civil War figures, including Gordon, Brown, Alexander Stephens, Robert Toombs, and Gov. Allen D. Candler, who lost an eye in the war.

There is also a marble statue of Benjamin Harvey Hill, a supporter of Jefferson Davis who, as a U.S. senator, played a role in influencing Pres. Rutherford B. Hayes to end Reconstruction. The statue was a factor in the 1886 gubernatorial election in Georgia. A. O. Bacon was the heavy favorite during the campaign, but the dedication of this monument drew John B. Gordon (the other candidate for the governorship), Jefferson Davis and his beloved daughter Winnie, and unexpectedly, James Longstreet. The sight caused such a frenzy in the hoards of the Confederate faithful in attendance that Gordon was swept into office. The monument formerly stood at the triangular Hardy Ivy Park at Peachtree and West Peachtree Streets.

In 1893 the funeral train of Jefferson Davis entered Georgia from New Orleans at West Point on May 29. Gov. William J. Northern and his staff boarded as an honor guard. In Atlanta the body was borne to the capitol where it lay in state for several hours before continuing the journey to Richmond.

The capitol occupies the site of Atlanta's first city hall (1854) and the Fulton County Courthouse, which survived the war but was demolished for the present structure. The Confederate flag had been first raised at the State Square on March 4, 1861. Union troops camped on the grounds. From here on September 6, 1864, Sherman evicted Atlanta's population, numbering 1,644, from the city.

One of history's better ironies is that Sherman had been one of the first train passengers to pass through Atlanta, then named Marthasville, when he was a young Army officer in 1844. He returned after the war on January 28, 1879, as commander in chief to inspect the area's military facilities. Sherman repeatedly praised the people of Atlanta for their progress since his wartime visit, visited the site where his protégé McPherson had died, attended a military ball at McPherson Barracks, and spoke with many officials, most of whom were former Confederate leaders like Joseph Brown and Alfred Colquitt. *Georgia State Museum of Science and Industry, State Capitol, Capitol Square (downtown), Washington Street Southwest and MLK Jr. Drive, Atlanta, GA 30334 (404) 656-2844.*

O'Reilly Monument. This monument at the southeastern corner of the city hall grounds honors Thomas Patrick O'Reilly, who earned the respect of both Confederates and Federals by ministering to all. As pastor of Immaculate Conception Church, the courageous O'Reilly persuaded Union Gen. Henry W. Slocum to spare the city hall, the courthouse, and four churches when the city was put to the torch in November 1864. This is the site of Sherman's headquarters, the Neal House, during the occupation, and from here Sherman started for Savannah. Thomas was quartered in the Austin Leydon House, which stood on Peachtree, and Schofield and Slocum roomed nearby. *68 Mitchell Street, across from the Capitol.*

Downtown Atlanta

On February 16, 1861, after resigning his seat in the Senate, Jefferson Davis, while traveling from Washington to the secession convention in Montgomery, Alabama, spoke to a large crowd during a stop at the depot at Marietta and Union. He was then the chief guest at a reception held in the Trent House, which stood on the corner of Decatur and Pryor.

As battles raged in Tennessee, thousands of casualties were delivered by rail to Atlanta. A general hospital was established at the Fair Ground (now the intersection of Memorial and Flat Shoals), and a convalescent camp was set up at Marietta and Ponder. The Gate City Hotel, between Marietta and Ponder, became a distributing hospital.

The Georgia Railroad roundhouse, a prominent landmark destroyed by Sherman, stood between the Washington Street Bridge and Piedmont Avenue.

Shrine of the Immaculate Conception (1873). This church replaced the 1848 original, which was demolished after the war. Father Thomas Patrick O'Reilly is buried in a basement crypt, which is open by appointment. *48 Martin Luther King Jr. Drive, Southwest, opposite World of Coca-Cola, Atlanta, GA 30303 (404) 521-1866.*

Rhodes Memorial Hall (1903). One of Georgia's least known but most spectacular Civil War attractions is found here. Three beautiful Tiffany stained-glass windows, made for Amos Giles Rhodes by the Von Gerichten Art Glass Company at a cost of forty thousand dollars, depict the rise and fall of the Confederacy. The first window illustrates the formation of the new government at Montgomery, Alabama. The second depicts the initial Southern victory at Manassas. The third pictures the final chapter of the war at Appomattox. Popular legend contends that Rhodes demanded that the Manassas scenes be reworked because he felt the Federals were not fleeing in sufficient panic. The windows and a staircase where they are placed were housed for years at the Georgia Department of Archives and History for safekeeping. They have been reconstructed in their full impressive glory at the restored Rhodes Hall, which is headquarters for the Georgia Trust for Historic Preservation. The building is inter-esting itself. Rhodes returned from a tour of European castles with a desire for an Americanized version for himself. The Victorian Romanesque Revival house of Stone Mountain granite was designed by Willis F. Denny. *Georgia Trust for Historic Preservation, 1516 Peachtree Street (Rhodes Hall), Atlanta, GA 30309 (404) 881-9950.*

The Road to Tara Museum. This new facility concentrates on the book and movie versions of *Gone with the Wind* but contains Atlanta campaign material in a war exhibit. *659 Peachtree Street, The Georgian Terrace, Atlanta, GA 30308 (404) 897-1939.*

Atlanta Museum. An extensive collection of Civil War artifacts is displayed in this combination museum-antique shop. *537 Peachtree Street, Northeast, Atlanta, GA 30309 (404) 872-8233.*

Peace Statue. This deeply moving monument depicts a winged angel imploring a Confederate infantryman to lower his weapon, symbolizing reconciliation. The figures, nine feet high and eight feet wide, stand atop a nine-foot-tall granite base. The bronze, by New York sculptor Allen G. Newman, was given to the city in 1911 by the Gate City Guard. It had been inspired by a peace mission the Guard had made to Union cities in 1879, and most of the cost was raised in the North. Following a parade of four thousand people, the monument was dedicated in front of fifty thousand. *Piedmont Park at the Fourteenth Street entrance.*

Johnston Headquarters Monument. This 1936 WPA memorial, consisting of fifty-five cannonballs, marks the site of Johnston's headquarters, the Nelson House, when he was relieved of command on July 17, 1864. *In front of the Mead Paper Company at 950 West Marietta Street, Northwest.*

At Marietta and Northside is the spot where Atlanta's mayor, James Williams, surrendered the city.

Old Lamppost. This is Atlanta's only 1855 gas lamp still standing in its original position. According to tradition, a hole in the base was caused by the explosion of a Union shell during the siege that killed Solomon Luckie. *Corner of Peachtree and Alabama, at the Five Points MARTA station.*

The siege of Atlanta began with a 20-pound Parrott shell fired by John Logan's Twentieth Corps that killed an unidentified little girl at Ivy and Ellis on July 20.

Welcome South Visitors Center. This new facility includes a display describing the Civil War battlefields preserved in Georgia and another about the siege and destruction of Atlanta. *200 Spring Street, Northwest, Atlanta, GA 30303 (404) 224-2023.*

Underground Atlanta. This was the heart of Atlanta's business district during the war. Most of the buildings along Alabama and Pryor Streets were destroyed during the siege. A temporary Confederate hospital was set up at those streets, today occupied by the Georgia Grande General Emporium. The overflow was treated in a park in the center of town, a dramatic scene depicted in *Gone with the Wind*.

The Underground is one of Atlanta's foremost attractions. On Upper Alabama Street, between Pryor and Central, is Atlanta Heritage Row. Glass windows etched with the likenesses of Joseph E. Johnston, Margaret Mitchell, and Scarlett O'Hara welcome visitors, who then pass through a linear presentation of Atlanta's history from its founding to the present. The Civil War display is centered around a recreated bombproof. Outside, a young soldier huddles in a corner while, inside, the figure of a girl, Carrie Berry, prays with hands folded. Carrie survived the forty-four-day siege and left a journal of her experiences, excerpts of which are read to the background sounds of bombardment. A fifteen-minute audiovisual program also illustrates Atlanta's Civil War fate. *Atlanta Heritage Row, Underground Atlanta, 55 Upper Alabama Street, Pryor and Alabama Streets, Atlanta, GA 30303 (404) 584-7879.*

The Phoenix. Officially titled *Atlanta from the Ashes* or *Rising Phoenix,* this eighteen-foot-high 1969 bronze sculpture by Italian artist Gamba Quirino was unveiled as a symbol of Atlanta's rise from the ashes of defeat after the Civil War. It was donated by the Rich Foundation on the one hundredth anniversary of the founding of Rich's Department Store. *Now in Woodruff Park at Five Points.*

Candler Building (1904). Over the grand staircase are marble portraits of John B. Gordon, Joseph Wheeler, Gov. Charles J. Jenkins,

Joel Chandler Harris, Eli Whitney, and poet Sidney Lanier. *127 Peachtree Street, Northeast.*

Atlanta University. The largest collection of Lincoln material in the South is in the Lincoln Room at Trevor Arnett Library, consisting of letters, books, pamphlets, and photographs. The material is available for scholarly research, and artifacts are displayed on special occasions.

Federal Reserve Bank of Atlanta. Displays of Confederate currency and state bank notes are in its Monetary Museum. *104 Marietta Street, Northwest, Atlanta, GA 30303 (404) 521-8764.*

Because Sherman burned all but four hundred of four thousand buildings in Atlanta, few original structures remain. Near Oglethorpe University, at the intersection of Peachtree Road and Ashford-Dunwoody Road, is Southlook (1856), once part of a great plantation and now the clubhouse of the Peachtree Golf Club. It was used as Sherman's headquarters July 18–19, 1864. Brookhaven, the Solomon Goodwin House (3967 Peachtree Road, 1831), was a landmark during the Atlanta campaign and bears scars from skirmishes. Legend claims that it was spared the torch by a loyal servant. Brookhaven was visited by Jefferson Davis, Alexander Stephens, and John B. Gordon.

Fort McPherson

Skirmishes were fought on the grounds of what is now Fort McPherson during the battle for Atlanta. Within the military installation named for the Federal general killed at Atlanta are several reminders of Confederate generals: a building named for Hardee, a gate named for Iverson, and roads named for Wheeler and Hood. The facility was established before the Civil War as a militia drilling ground, and Confederate soldiers were trained here. Barracks and a cartridge factory were constructed then burned during Hood's retreat. McPherson became headquarters for the Third Militia District, which ruled Georgia during Reconstruction. Union Gens. George Meade and John Pope were stationed here. *West of U.S. 29 between Atlanta and East Point, where Atlanta's southernmost fortifications ended.*

South and West Fulton County

McCook's cavalry crossed the Chattahoochee River six miles south of Campbellton, then rode through Palmetto to destroy track on the Atlanta and West Point Railroad. At Fayetteville they destroyed a Confederate wagon train, butchering the horses and mules, then destroyed more track at Lovejoy and were chased through Fayetteville to Newnan.

When Sherman shifted most of his forces southwest of Atlanta to converge at Jonesboro, he sent Oliver O. Howard (replacing McPherson) west through Campbellton and Fairburn. In the center was Thomas's Army of the Cumberland, which passed through Ben Hill and Red Oak, on U.S. 29 south of College Park, breaking up rails between there and Fairburn. Schofield took an inside route through Red Oak to Rough and Ready.

At the northern edge of Riverdale is the log Drew Couch House, headquarters for Sherman and Thomas in August 1864.

Rough and Ready Tavern

Now called Mountain View, Rough and Ready was visited by Union cavalry during an 1864 raid. Confederates marched through en route to the decisive conflict at Jonesboro, and Schofield's men cut the Macon Railroad here. After Atlanta's surrender, its citizens were evacuated to this point by Sherman's orders. *U.S. 19-41 between Hapeville and Forest Park, northeast of the intersection of GA 70 and GA 92.*

Campbellton

In front of Campbellton Baptist Church is a UDC-WPA monument erected in 1937 marking the site of the old Campbell County Courthouse (the Depression forced Campbell to merge with Fulton). It commemorates the devotion of Capt. T. C. Glover, a delegate to Georgia's secession convention. He raised a company and led it to Virginia, where he died at Winchester on September 9, 1864. In 1867 his wife, Elizabeth, asked survivors of Company A, Twenty-first Georgia Infantry, to hold an annual reunion here to remember their fallen comrades. They honored her request for many years, starting the long tradition of Confederate reunions. The Latham

House (1829) and Masonic Lodge, both still standing, were hit by artillery fire during the siege of Atlanta.

The Methodist church cemetery has a section of Confederate soldiers who died fighting in the area. A Union soldier is buried in the Bullard family cemetery. He was wounded in a July 4, 1864, skirmish and died in the Bullard home. The grave was recently marked. *Campbellton is northeast of the intersection of GA 70 and GA 92.*

Fairburn

In the city cemetery on U.S. 29 just west of town, a twenty-foot-high column, surrounded by an iron fence, honors Confederate veterans. It is an unusual Southern memorial donated by Col. Samuel Tate of the Pickens County marble quarries. At the railroad station on U.S. 29, a plaque mounted by the UDC on a brick base (1937) marks the spot where the first Confederate flag in the state was unfurled on March 4, 1861. The design had been approved the day before in Montgomery, Alabama, and the returning delegates and their wives stopped the Atlanta and West Point train in Grantville to purchase fabric. They had crafted a flag by the time they reached Fairburn, and it flew from the train until they arrived in Atlanta. It

Fairburn's beautiful Confederate memorial was made from Tate, Georgia, marble.

was in Fairburn that the Army of the Tennessee, on its way to Jonesboro, cut the West Point Railroad.

Palmetto

In July 1864 Federal cavalry raiders burned the depot and two trains, then tore up seven miles of track. Beside the old railroad station on U.S. 29, a fifteen-foot draped obelisk was erected in 1906 to mark the area where the Army of Tennessee camped on September 19, 1864, following the fall of Atlanta. When Jefferson Davis addressed the troops on September 21, the battle-weary veterans were rude and demanded that Johnston be returned to command. Davis did not make the change, and Hood crossed the Chattahoochee at Pumkintown Ferry to begin his ill-fated Tennessee campaign.

Jonesboro

After an ineffective month-long siege, Sherman abandoned his trenches surrounding Atlanta and struck south to destroy the two remaining railroads. If Hood's supplies were cut off, he would have to abandon the city, so the Confederate commander sent half his force under the command of William J. Hardee to protect the railroad at Jonesboro. On August 31 a Confederate attack on the Federal lines was shattered, and a massed Union assault the next day nearly overran the Confederate line, forcing Hardee's retreat to Lovejoy. After destroying supplies he could not transport, Hood left Atlanta that night and joined Hardee. Sherman entered Atlanta the following day. Confederates and Federals faced each other at Lovejoy for several days, but no combat resulted. The Atlanta campaign ended here, and in November Judson Kilpatrick's horsemen drove out Wheeler's cavalry to clear the way for the Fifteenth and Seventeenth Corps at the start of Sherman's march. Jonesboro was nearly destroyed by cavalry raids and the battle. During Sherman's occupation foragers stripped the land of provisions, leaving the citizens destitute.

Hardee marched through the night to Jonesboro along GA 138, through East Point and Rough and Ready. His attack on the first day struck the Federal line just west of Jonesboro, on both sides of GA

138 near the Flint River. Hardee retreated to hastily constructed defensive works on the western and northern edges of the town, at the railroad depot near the Confederate cemetery.

Patrick Cleburne Confederate Cemetery. Named for the general who fought here and died months later at Franklin, Tennessee, the cemetery contains the graves of hundreds of Southerners who fell in the battle. The Federals buried the dead, who had been left on this field, in two mass graves. Individual stones marked "Unknown" were erected by the state in 1892 when eight hundred to one thousand casualties were reinterred. The stones are placed to form a Confederate battle flag. The cemetery has a large stone entrance arch with embedded cannonballs, and in the center of the grounds is a monument honoring the fallen, dedicated on April 26, 1933. *On GA 54 at the northern edge of Jonesboro.*

Historic Jonesboro, Inc. (P.O. Box 922, Jonesboro, GA 30237 [770] 478-6549) has opened a museum in the Old Jail (Clayton County History Center, 123 King Street, 1869), displaying artifacts from both armies, including a Bible that stopped a Yankee bullet from piercing a Rebel heart. Stately Oaks, an 1839 plantation house, has also been restored (Stately Oaks Plantation Home and Historic Community, 100 Carriage Lane at Jodeco Road, P.O. Box 922, Jonesboro, GA 30237 [770] 473-0197), which was a landmark for Sherman's armies. Each October, during the Jonesboro Fall Festival and Battle Reenactment, many activities are held at Stately Oaks, which hosts a Tara Ball. A visitors center at 9712 Tara Boulevard distributes an excellent driving tour of Jonesboro and Clayton County.

The Warren House (102 West Mimosa Drive, 1859) was headquarters and hospital for both armies during the battle of Jonesboro, August 31–September 1. Illinois troops captured the house, and the signatures of the Union soldiers are still readable on the interior walls. The Johnson-Blalock House (155 North Street, 1840) was home to James F. Johnson, a member of the state secession convention. The structure was a hospital during the battle and served as a Confederate commissary warehouse. At the Stephen Carnes House (154 North McDonough Street, 1850s) wagons and caskets were

made for the Confederacy. The rear half of the Waldrop-Brown-
Edwards House (158 South Main Street, 1860s) was destroyed
during the battle; the home had been used as a hospital. At Pope
Dickson and Son Funeral Home (168 North McDonough Street,
1850s) is the hearse that transported Alexander Stephens's body to
his grave in 1883.

The 1867 depot at 104 North Main Street replaced the original
wooden depot burned by Union Gen. Judson Kilpatrick in August
1864. The 1869 courthouse-Masonic lodge (144 North McDonough Street) occupies the same foundation as its predecessor, and
the stone depot and jail (both from 1869) replace those that Kilpatrick torched. Most of the downtown business area was also
destroyed by rampaging cavalry, although the brick exteriors are
original.

The Allen-Carnes House (1820; the oldest structure in Clayton
County), the Abner-Camp Plantation (Lake Jodeco Road, 1840),
and other country homes became refuges for Jonesboro citizens
fleeing the two days of fighting, August 31–September 1. After the
defeat, Hood assembled the disorganized remnants of the Army of
Tennessee at the Crawford-Talmadge Plantation (1835; on U.S. 19
five miles south of Jonesboro), now called Lovejoy Plantation. Skirmishes were fought nearby. Legend holds that this plantation was
the inspiration for Twelve Oaks in *Gone with the Wind.* Many houses
in Georgia claim that honor, but Margaret Mitchell spent several
summers in this area with her grandmother, listening to the stories
of elderly residents who remembered the war. She researched the
book at the Clayton County Courthouse, and Jonesboro figures
prominently in the narrative. The owner of Lovejoy possesses the
movie facade of Tara.

Sigma Chi Monument. Seven Confederates gathered near here
after the fall of Atlanta and contemplated the probable Confederate
defeat. Wondering if their common university fraternity would survive in the South, they organized the Constantine Chapter of Sigma
Chi. In 1939 this ten-ton Georgia white marble monument was
erected to recognize their devotion. *At 11001 Tara Boulevard (U.S.
41), between Jonesboro and Griffin.*

Lovejoy

Near the cemetery behind the burned ruins of the historic Crawford-Dorsey House are earthworks built for the defense of the Army of Tennessee after its retreat from Jonesboro. Cavalry skirmishes were fought here in November 1864 as Sherman began his March to the Sea. Permission to visit must be obtained from the Clayton Water Authority. *At the corner of McDonough and Freeman Roads, one-half mile north of GA 3 near U.S. 19.*

Douglasville

A Confederate monument on the courthouse lawn was dedicated on April 26, 1914.

New Manchester

Industry developed very early along the swift rapids of Sweetwater Creek. By 1864 a seventeen-building mill community of sixty employees was daily manufacturing 750 yards of cloth for Confederate uniforms, tents, powder bags, and blankets. A flour and grist-mill and a leather factory were also functioning. After Johnston abandoned the Chattahoochee River line, Union cavalry under Lt. Col. Silas Adams and Maj. Haviland Thompkin occupied New Manchester on July 2. They soon burned the thirty houses in the town, a warehouse, the commissary, and a five-story mill, then brought up a battery of 12-pounder Napoleons to pound down the three-hundred-foot-long wooden mill dam. Two other mills on the creek—Ferguson-Merchant to the north and Alexander's to the south—were also destroyed. The predominately female work force and their dependents, about five hundred people, joined the women from Roswell and were dispatched to work in Northern mills.

The site is preserved in Sweetwater Creek State Park, where footpaths lead beside the old mill race to the dramatic ruins of the factory. Archaeological excavation has revealed bolts of intact fabric and hundreds of machine parts. Large machinery was salvaged during World War II scrap-metal drives. *West of Atlanta, off the Thornton Road exit of I-20; Sweetwater Creek State Park, P.O.*

Box 816, Mount Vernon Road, Lithia Springs, GA 30057 (770) 732-5871.

DeKalb County

Decatur

When the battle of Atlanta began, Union troops had circled east of the city to cut the Augusta Railroad. As Hood attacked McPherson, Wheeler's Confederate cavalry attacked McPherson's wagon train in Decatur. Initially successful, the assault was recalled when Hood's action failed. An engraved stone on the campus of Agnes Scott College indicates the main scene of the battle, and a second stone at the old courthouse records further fighting that day. A draped granite obelisk on the grounds honors DeKalb's Confederate veterans. The original monument fell and broke while being erected in 1907. On the first day of the infamous March to the Sea, Henry W. Slocum's left wing, with Sherman present, marched out of Atlanta on the Decatur Road and passed through town, destroying considerable property.

The old courthouse now houses the DeKalb Historical Society, which has assembled an impressive exhibit titled "Johnny Reb and

The old DeKalb County Courthouse houses an impressive Civil War museum.

Billy Yank: The Life of the Common Soldier." The society has also restored several important Civil War–era houses (The Historic Complex of DeKalb Historical Society, 720 West Trinity Place, Decatur, GA 30030 [404] 373-1088), including the Swanton House, which was used as headquarters by several Federal generals and where shot from the battle is still embedded in the walls, and the Mary Gay House, home of a heroine who refused to evacuate her home when Union troops occupied the town. Gay later picked up bullets and shells to exchange for food. After the war she wrote a book describing her trials, *Life in Dixie During the War,* which Margaret Mitchell used for reference. Battle swirled around the houses, but they escaped destruction then and in November 1864 when Federals were inspired by the burning of Atlanta the previous night. *DeKalb Historical Society Museum, Old Courthouse on the Square, 101 Court Square, Decatur, GA 30030 (404) 373-1088.*

Women gathered daily at Mason's Corner, the intersection of Clairmont Avenue and Ponce de Leon Avenue, to sew uniforms for a regiment of local men, the DeKalb Light Infantry. On Sycamore Street is High House, where Sherman is thought to have watered his horse at an ivy-covered well.

In the city cemetery on Commerce Drive near Barry Street is a six-foot cruciform tablet erected in 1984 to honor Decatur's Confederate dead. Mary Gay is buried here. Nearby is an Italian marble obelisk, slipped through the blockade, marking the grave of Charles Murphy, who died before he could serve as a delegate to Georgia's secession convention. He had expressed the hope that he would not live to see Georgia leave the Union, and he did not.

Tucker

Browning Courthouse was also known as Tucker Militia District 572 Courthouse. This one-room white clapboard structure (1860) was a landmark during the battle of Atlanta. It is thought to have been appropriated as Sherman's headquarters or by other Union officials during the raid to destroy the Stone Mountain depot on July 18, 1864. Used by a justice of the peace until January 1977, it was threatened by road construction until relocated and placed on a foundation of stones from an old mill. *4898 LaVista Road, in front of the Tucker Recreation Center.*

Stone Mountain

Stone Mountain Cemetery. Buried here in a plot are 150 unknown soldiers who died in local hospitals or in skirmishes with Union cavalry under Kenner Garrard who raided the county on July 18. The depot and much of the community, then named New Gibralter, were burned, including a tower atop the big rock. *In the city cemetery on Main Street, at the northern end of the business district.*

The Stillwell House. The house (Ridge Avenue and Mountain Street), a tourist inn, was a Confederate hospital during the war. Visitors should stop at Stone Mountain Relics and Civil War Museum (968 Main Street [770] 469-1425) and Stone Mountain Village Museum (941 Main Street [770] 469-8045).

Stone Mountain Park

Certainly ranking among the greatest memorial efforts in the world is the famous Stone Mountain carving. The mountain itself is imposing, rising abruptly 825 feet above the surrounding countryside and covering 580 acres. At the beginning of his Savannah campaign, Sherman and half of his army marveled at the granite monolith. They could not have imagined that an incredible Confederate monument would be initiated here fifty-two years later.

In 1916 sculptor Gutzon Borglum, who had made bronze figures of Lincoln and Union Gen. Philip Sheridan, began work on a grand plan: seven large figures of Confederate leaders followed by an army of one thousand men, representing all branches of the service and marching from the depths of the mountain. The image would measure twelve hundred feet by thirteen hundred, and at the base of the mountain a memorial hall, three hundred feet long and fifty feet wide, would be carved out of the hard granite. Unfortunately, World War I and a lack of funds slowed his work. By 1925 Borglum had only completed Lee's head when he argued with the organizing officials, destroyed his plans and model, and left Georgia. He later supervised the work at Mount Rushmore.

His successor, Augustus Lukeman, chiseled off Lee's head and started over, but when money ran out in 1928, only Lee's head had been recarved. Visitors marveled at the famed head for thirty-six years. In 1958 Georgia bought the mountain and created the Stone Mountain Memorial Association, which resumed the work in 1964. A scaled-down version of the original plan—three mounted figures of Robert E. Lee, his invaluable lieutenant Thomas J. "Stonewall" Jackson, and Jefferson Davis—was completed in 1972 by Walker Hancock.

It is difficult to imagine the size of the figures from below. This sculpture, the world's largest, covers three acres and is 90 feet by 190 feet. The figures are four hundred feet above the ground and are recessed forty-two feet into the mountainside. A replica of the *General* offers visitors a train ride around the base of the mountain.

At the viewing pavilion below Stone Mountain are two statues: Valor, a young soldier with a broken sword, and Sacrifice, a grieving woman and child. Facing the carving is Memorial Hall, which houses a good Civil War museum. On summer nights dazzling laser shows play over the face of the mountain.

The main building in the park, Confederate Hall, contains a two-part display titled "The War in Georgia." In the lobby is a comprehensive pictorial exhibit of the Atlanta campaign, and in an adjoining chamber is an impressive diorama illustrating all the Civil War activity that occurred in Georgia. Rivers, mountains, cities, armies, and trains are faithfully recreated, and lights illustrate the bombardment of Fort Pulaski, the Great Locomotive Chase, the Atlanta campaign, and the March to the Sea as a taped narrative describes each event. Also displayed are large figures of Confederate heroes created by Rich's Department Store during the Civil War centennial of the early 1960s.

In the park's antebellum plantation, which consists of pre–Civil War structures assembled from across the state, is the Thomas R. R. Cobb House. Cobb made considerable contributions to Georgia's legal system, helped write the Confederate Constitution, and died a general at Fredericksburg. The house, transported from Athens, will be a bed and breakfast inn. *Georgia's Stone*

Mountain Park, Highway 78, P.O. Box 778, Stone Mountain, GA 30086 (770) 498-5702.

Belmont

Federal cavalry under Kenner Garrard retreated from Flat Rock (Flat Shoals) and were bottled up here by Wheeler. *On U.S. 278 east of I-285.*

4

Northeast Georgia

EXCEPT FOR RAIDS by Federal cavalry, northeast Georgia escaped destruction during the war. There were few large plantations or slave owners, and the men of the region were just as likely to fight for the Confederacy as they were to evade the draft or to desert or to serve the Union. Bandits roamed the region, terrorizing isolated farms and small communities, forcing Gov. Joseph Brown to dispatch patrols periodically to suppress the anarchy, a largely useless effort in the mountainous wilderness.

Pickens, Dawson, and Cherokee Counties were Unionist strongholds troubled by guerrilla groups like McCallum's Scouts, a collection of outlaws, renegades, and deserters. Food production suffered, and wide-scale hunger was commonplace. Returning Southern soldiers hunted down the renegades, resulting in feuds that continued for decades.

Jefferson Davis began his flight through Georgia along the southern edge of this area. He was accompanied by two separate treasures: the Confederacy treasury and deposits of several Richmond banks.

The region was home to many Civil War notables, including Alexander Stephens, Robert Toombs, and the Cobb brothers. The area is often called the "Classic South" for its abundance of fine antebellum homes, many preserved in beautiful communities.

Murray County

An expedition to clear the mountains of guerrillas in April 1865 left one Confederate officer dead. He was buried at the Spring Place

Cemetery, where a young Union soldier also rests. In 1864 residents found a sixteen-year-old boy dead in a barn, and in 1976 the local American Legion Post gave the Federal a headstone that reads "Little Unknown Soldier."

Pickens County

To protest Georgia's secession from the Union, local citizens raised the American flag in 1861 and flew it for a month. Men from this region served in both armies. Many Confederate memorials are made of Pickens County marble. Although beautiful, they erode quickly; hard Elberton granite is preferred.

Canton

Georgia's Civil War governor, Joseph Brown, taught in Canton while studying law and later opened a practice here before entering politics. When he died in 1894 his heirs presented the city with a parcel of land near his old home to establish Brown Park. The park has a beautiful Confederate monument, a marble arch, dedicated on Confederate Memorial Day 1903, and a monument to Brown, erected in 1906 by his three children. The business district of Canton was burned by Federals in October 1864, apparently in retaliation for Confederate cavalry raids.

Union County

Georgia's most recent Civil War monument and one of the most unusual was unveiled on November 11, 1995, in Blairsville. The seventeen-foot-tall black granite memorial is divided into seven steps, each inscribed with the names of citizens killed in a war, including Native Americans from battles with settlers. Of the 158 total, 98 were Confederate and 3 Federal, although many men enlisted in the Union army in nearby Tennessee. The inscription is from Shakespeare's *Henry V:* "But we . . . shall be remembered, we few, we happy few, we band of brothers; for he today that sheds his blood with me shall be my brother."

Dahlonega

The U.S. Mint established here in 1837 was seized by the Confederates in 1861. Finding that minting coins was too expensive, government officials sent $23,716 in gold and silver bullion to the Confederate Treasury. By the end of the war the machinery was so damaged that the mint was closed and the property donated to North Georgia College. The building burned in 1878, and the site is occupied by the Price Memorial Building, its steeple gilded in Dahlonega gold.

Shakerag

In 1864 a skirmish erupted in this Forsyth County community between Unionist guerrillas and the Eighth Texas Rangers. One Confederate, James Street, was killed; he was buried in Shady Grove Church cemetery.

Habersham County

On October 12, 1864, Confederate cavalry turned back Federal troopers in a sharp clash known as the battle of Narrows (or the battle of Currahee, a nearby mountain). The victory saved a ripe harvest from destruction.

In response to Gov. Joseph Brown's request, blacksmith Edwin Williams set to work on Sautee Creek manufacturing pikes, a stopgap weapon consisting of a long wooden staff with a bayonet attached. Stored in warehouses in Augusta and Charleston, many were sent home by Federal occupiers as unique souvenirs. Joe Brown pikes are prized exhibits in Georgia's Confederate museums.

Toccoa

A Confederate monument was unveiled on the courthouse grounds in 1922.

Gainesville

Gen. James Longstreet (1821–1904), one of Lee's finest commanders, was born in Augusta and made his last home here. Called by Lee

"My Old Warhorse," Longstreet served at First Manassas, Seven Days, Second Manassas, Antietam, Fredericksburg, Gettysburg, and was the hero in his native Georgia at Chickamauga. Severely wounded in the Wilderness, he returned for Petersburg and Appomattox. Pres. Ulysses Grant, whose wife was Longstreet's cousin, appointed him to a variety of civil service jobs, including that of superintendent of revenue and postmaster at Gainesville, where he also ran a hotel, planted a vineyard, and wrote his memoirs, *From Manassas to Appomattox*. Following Lee's death, Virginia generals conspired to blame Longstreet for the defeat at Gettysburg and the subsequent loss of the war. His real sin, however, was joining the Republican Party, advocating suffrage for blacks, and leading them against a postwar New Orleans insurrection by whites.

Longstreet's grave is in Alta Vista Cemetery at North Avenue and Fourth, off Jesse Jewell Parkway. A large stone monument, with crossed U.S. and Confederate flags, lists his extensive service for both nations. Buried beside him is his first wife, Marie Louise, who died here in 1889. During the war they lost four children to disease. Longstreet's second wife, Helen Dortch (when they married she was thirty-four, he seventy-six), gained fame during World War II by working in a bomber factory in Marietta at the age of eighty-one. She died in 1961 in Milledgeville and is buried there.

Also buried here are two Georgia governors who served as Confederate officers. James Milton Smith was a delegate to the Confederate Congress, and Allen Daniel Candler compiled Georgia's Confederate records.

A small stone monument on Park Hill Drive marks the site of Longstreet's original homeplace and vineyards. Longstreet's Piedmont Hotel, long thought destroyed, has been identified on Maple, and there are plans to restore it. Woodrow Wilson worked on his doctoral thesis there, and renowned Georgia newsman Henry Grady helped Longstreet write his memoirs. The Longstreet Society has prepared a tour of six sites associated with the general, including Helen's house, where the couple probably lived, at 746 Green Street, and the old post office, replaced by a federal courthouse. *P.O. Box 191, Gainesville, GA 30503.*

The Georgia Mountains Museum has exhibits concerning Longstreet. *311 Green Street, Gainesville, GA 30501 (770) 536-0889; 534-6080.*

A statue fondly called "Old Joe" was erected to veterans of the Cause on June 7, 1909, on the public square at Washington and Main Streets. A devastating tornado in 1910 sent a statue of Col. C. C. Sanders crashing to the ground; the figure was seated in a chair supported by eight-foot-high columns. Residents are attempting to round up all the pieces and put Colonel Sanders together again.

On the third floor of the federal courthouse at 121 Spring Street Southeast (the former post office) is a 1936 WPA mural titled *Morgan's Raiders.*

Redwine Church (1845). The Seventeenth Georgia of Colquitt's Brigade was one of the most famous units in the Confederate army. It had been organized here in 1861. The Seventeenth fought with distinction in every campaign of the Army of Northern Virginia and surrendered with Johnston in North Carolina. A stone monument honoring the men of the brigade is on the church grounds. Local soldiers mustered here for service in the war. *Redwine Methodist Church, south of Gainesville on Poplar Springs Road (SR 332).*

Gwinnett County

Thomas Maguire's journal describes life on his one-thousand-acre plantation, Promised Land (1820), during Sherman's March to the Sea. While Maguire hid in the woods, Federal soldiers slaughtered his livestock and burned his gin house, barn, stables, and fences. The plantation home is at the intersection of Lee Road and GA 124.

On Truckum Road is the plantation house called Little Egypt (1820), which was the Civil War home of Robert and Nancy Craig. Tradition claims they foresaw the war and the economic havoc it would play, so they stored grain in hidden sites. Sherman missed the caches of foodstuffs, and for several years people from Georgia and surrounding states came to buy grain and cotton from the Craigs.

One of Georgia's most recent monuments, dedicated September 12, 1993, in downtown Lawrenceville, has a modern look, distinguishing it from all the statues and obelisks that have been erected during the last 130 years. It is dedicated to the Confederate veterans of Gwinnett County.

Walton County

Monroe

A Confederate monument dedicated in 1907 stands on the courthouse square. In Walma Knight Memorial Park Cemetery, a block east of the courthouse at Broad and State Streets, is a statue of Capt. Matthew Talbot Nunnaly, who was killed at Gettysburg and probably buried in Richmond or Savannah. The memorial was placed by his sister, Mary Nunnaly Sadridge.

Social Circle

Because of its important railroad facilities, this Walton County community was visited twice by the Federals. In July 1864 the railroad was destroyed to interrupt Hood's communications with Augusta. On November 17 Sherman's left wing camped nearby and destroyed the railroad from Social Circle to Madison on the following day.

At the southern edge of town on GA 11 is a small monument to Emma Sansom. Sansom, born in Social Circle, was a teenager in northeastern Alabama when she braved enemy fire to show Nathan Bedford Forrest a ford across a creek, enabling him to thwart Col. A. D. Streight's 1863 cavalry raid into Georgia. The act made Sansom a Southern heroine. (*See pages 27–28.*)

Loganville

Marauding Federals stole the city charter in 1864. It was found by some fishermen in a stream some distance away.

Barrow County

Winder

The final destruction by Sherman's cavalry during the Atlanta campaign occurred on August 3, 1864, five miles northwest of Winder at King's Tanyard. Two brigades that escaped from

Sunshine Church in Jones County intended to resupply in Athens but turned west when they encountered resistance. One brigade reached Federal lines, but troopers under Col. Horace Capron were surprised by Confederate cavalry. Capron lost 430 men to the Southerners; he and 6 men reached Sherman on foot. The site is just southeast of the intersection of GA 11 and County Line–Auburn Road.

A small granite monument honoring the unknown Confederate dead stands at Triangle Park in Rosehill Cemetery. One Confederate killed at Jug Tavern was reburied here in 1907. Extensive research initiated by a relative in 1971 identified the man as Martin Van Buren Parkhurst of Kentucky. He had been purposefully buried near the spring of a local Unionist.

Rockwell Universalist Church (1839; present picturesque building 1881) was the site of a Confederate training camp. *East side of GA 53 North at Rockwell Church Road.*

Bethlehem United Methodist Church (1790; present building 1949) was a mustering spot for area troops, and the local women sewed clothing for the soldiers at an arbored campground. *South of Winder on GA 11, then east on GA 324 and right at the next two crossroads to the church.*

Statham

This is the home of John C. Statham, who provided rent-free shelter to Civil War orphans and widows. North of Statham at GA 82 and Thurmond Road is the Thurmond House (1850), where the lady of the house gave baked goods to the passing soldiers.

Jefferson

A Confederate monument dedicated on Confederate Memorial Day 1911 stands on a traffic island in front of the Crawford Long Museum on GA 15. The stone base was originally topped by a statue of a soldier, but it was accidentally knocked off during the unveiling of the adjacent Crawford Long Monument in 1940 and replaced with a Maltese cross. The head of the statue and other pieces remain in the possession of local citizens.

Commerce

A large marble cenotaph honoring the men and women of the Confederacy was dedicated April 26, 1941, beside the railroad on U.S. 41 in Spencer Park.

Carnesville

Helen Longstreet, widow of Gen. James Longstreet, attended the dedication of this monument in 1910. The soldier statue has lost its rifle and faces the courthouse, his back to the community.

Homer

The historic Banks County Courthouse was completed in 1863, reportedly paid for with sixty-six hundred dollars in Confederate currency.

Athens

When New Orleans fell in 1862, Cook and Brother, an important armory for the Confederacy, relocated to Athens. Operated by two British engineers, W. C. Ferdinand and Francis L. Cook, the plant manufactured rifles and other military equipment. It was the largest private armory in the nation. The two men commanded a militia unit when Sherman began his march to Savannah. They fought bravely at Griswoldville and Savannah, where Cook was killed, but the factories continued to produce munitions until the end of the war.

Col. Horace Capron's retreating Union cavalry attempted to enter Athens in 1864, but the Georgia Militia destroyed the bridge over the Oconee River and placed artillery on a hill overlooking the river, forcing the Federals to withdraw.

University of Georgia. The University of Georgia, closed when most of its students joined the Confederate army, reopened in 1868 with many student veterans and a special program for maimed soldiers. During the war, university buildings were used to house refugees and wounded soldiers.

Every year on Confederate Memorial Day (April 26, except when it falls on a Sunday) a climate-controlled vault is unlocked in the main library (third floor, Hargrett Rare Books and Manuscripts Library [706] 542-0626), and a fragile, twelve-foot-long vellum scroll is carefully extracted from a lead-lined copper tube. On that scroll is the original handwritten Constitution of the Confederate States of America. The priceless artifact was included with other government documents that accompanied Jefferson Davis when Richmond was evacuated. The trainload of papers was abandoned in Chester, South Carolina, where a newspaper reporter, Felix G. DeFontaines, recovered a portion, including the Constitution. It passed into the hands of Mrs. George DeRenne of Savannah and was donated to the university in 1938.

Much of the Constitution was written by Thomas R. R. Cobb, an Athens resident and legal scholar who earned the highest grades ever recorded at the university. As a Confederate general, he was mortally wounded while commanding Georgians at the famed stone wall and sunken road at Fredericksburg on December 13, 1862, bleeding to death within sight of the house where his parents had been married. Athens closed for his funeral on December 17. His signature and that of Robert Toombs of nearby Washington are clearly distinguishable on the document.

On the second floor wall of the northwest corner of the Old College Building (1806; modeled after Yale's Connecticut Hall) is a plaque marking Alexander Stephens's 1832 dorm room, which he shared with Crawford W. Long, a pioneer of anesthesia.

Union soldiers stabled their horses in the ground floor of Phi Kappa Hall (1836) and held parties on the second floor after the war. Federals camped on campus and fired at the columns of the chapel. A sundial in front of the chapel marks the site of the Toombs Oak. Fiery Robert Toombs was expelled for a prank, and an apocryphal story has him returning for commencement and speaking so eloquently beneath the tree that everyone left the official ceremony to hear him.

In front of the university on College Avenue is a forty-foot-tall obelisk honoring the men who fought for the Confederacy. In Oconee Cemetery, directly behind Sanford Stadium, is a shaft

The world's only double-barreled cannon was built in Athens, but it was a dismal failure.

erected in memory of the Southern dead. It is surrounded by several Confederate graves.

Double-Barreled Cannon. This famous cannon was designed by a local man, John Gilleland, who was a Home Guard soldier and house builder. It was intended to fire two balls connected by an eight-foot-long chain, which was expected to mow down enemy troops. Tests, however, proved the weapon to be useless. The charges would not fire simultaneously, causing the chain to break and the balls to fly unpredictably. According to legend, a test firing killed a cow and destroyed the chimney of a cabin while a line of poles erected in front of the cannon to represent Federal infantry stood unscathed. The cannon was preserved as a curiosity and used to celebrate Democratic political victories. Replicas of the unique artifact are available for purchase at the local chamber of commerce. The cannon was cast at the Athens Foundry and Machine Works, which is now the John Gilleland Conference Center (1849), one of three structures in Athens History Village. *At City Hall, on the corner of College and Hancock.*

Thomas R. R. Cobb (1823–62), his brother Howell (1815–68), and two other Confederate generals, William M. Brown and Martin L. Smith, rest in Oconee Hill Cemetery. Brown (1823–83), appointed assistant secretary of state by Davis, was at the siege of Savannah. Smith (1819–66), West Point class of 1842, was a noted military engineer. A native New Yorker, Smith married a southerner and planned the defenses at New Orleans, Vicksburg (where he commanded until John Pemberton's arrival), and Mobile.

The Cobb House (425 Hill Street, 1851) was the Greek Revival home of Howell Cobb. As Speaker of the U.S. House, he was an important figure in the passage of the Compromise of 1850, which probably delayed the Civil War for a decade. After serving as Pres. James Buchanan's treasury secretary, Cobb was a leader in Georgia's secessionist movement, president of the Montgomery convention that established the Confederate States of America, president of the Confederate Provisional Congress, and a strong contender for the presidency of the Confederacy. He rose to the rank of major general and returned to Georgia to command the Georgia Militia and act as liaison between the Confederate government and Georgia's testy Governor Brown. He was one of five men the North wanted to punish after the war (two other Georgians, Alexander Stephens and Robert Toombs, also made the list). Cobb's first house (698 Poplar Street, 1835) is behind Emmanuel Church.

Lucy Cobb Institute (200 North Milledgeville Avenue), known for its intricate ironwork, was established in 1858 by Thomas R. R. Cobb to educate women. In 1855 Cobb had donated the pulpit furniture at First Presbyterian Church (185 East Hancock Street). His home was saved from demolition by being moved to Stone Mountain Park.

The President's House (University of Georgia, 570 Prince Avenue, 1858) was purchased by Benjamin Harvey Hill in 1867. Hill, who had been educated here and had married a local woman, established this residence while his sons attended the university. Afterward he moved to Atlanta and served in the U.S. House and Senate.

Gilmer Hall (Prince Street and Oglethorpe Avenue) was utilized as a Confederate hospital and rehabilitation center.

Watkinsville

After suffering defeat at Sunshine Church in August 1864, Federal cavalry rode through Watkinsville on their way to Athens. This was the home of Bishop Atticus Green Haywood, a missionary and Confederate chaplain. A Confederate monument, a plaque set on a stone, stands at the courthouse. Local legend holds that a Southern soldier on leave hid in the Eagle Tavern (late 1700s) while Union cavalry passed through. The tavern is now a welcome center on U.S. 441 and is listed on the National Register. *Watkinsville, GA 30677 (706) 769-5197.*

Lexington

A monument honoring Oglethorpe County's Confederate veterans was unveiled beside the courthouse on April 26, 1910. It has the longest inscription of any Confederate county monument, containing 768 names that must have included every person in the area.

Crawford

The town was designated a Confederate supply center as the war ended, and boxcars filled with quartermaster stores lined the track near the old depot, which is constructed of stone and railroad ties.

Greene County

Greensboro

The fifty unknown soldiers buried in a section of the city cemetery in northeastern Greensboro died in local hospitals. The Confederate statue on the courthouse lawn was erected in 1898 to honor the Confederate dead.

Union Point

A section of the city cemetery in northern Union Point contains seventeen graves of Confederates who died in military hospitals. On Sibley Street near the railroad tracks beside a bank, a WPA monument placed in 1936 marks the site of a wayside home tending to the needs of traveling or wounded soldiers in 1862–64. A bronze plaque on top of the hill overlooking the Georgia Railroad at the top of "The Big Steps" salutes fourteen women who operated the home and prepared more than fifty thousand meals for soldiers. Another monument commemorates the Third Georgia Regiment Reunion.

Local lore contends that, as part of the evacuation of Richmond, the heavy wagons used to transport the Confederate treasury bogged down in a swamp. The gold was allegedly buried one-quarter mile due east of Public Square (then Sunshine Church and now Bethesda), on GA 44 north of Daniel Springs, fourteen miles from Washington, Georgia.

White Plains

To raise money for the Confederacy, the good people here staged a play in 1861. A young actress, Laura Alfriend, wearing a paper costume on a stage lit by candles, burned to death in a tragic accident. Her grave in the community cemetery states that she lost her life "aiding the cause of the Confederacy."

Hartwell

Hart County's Confederate monument dedicated in 1908 stands beside the courthouse.

Elberton

Local women donated their silk dresses to Richmond for use in the creation of an observation balloon. Known as "the Granite Capital of the World," Elberton was the manufacturing center for many Confederate monuments found in Georgia and throughout the South. The story of the city's first monument is told in the Granite Museum. Created by Arthur Beter, an immigrant who had never seen a Confederate soldier, the eight-foot statue was erected in 1898 in Sutton Square. The local people thought the squatty mustachioed figure clad in a Union overcoat and cap looked like a Yankee and nicknamed it "Dutchy." It lasted only twenty-five months (longer than Beter, who soon departed). On August 14, 1900, a mob knocked Dutchy from his pedestal (an empty whiskey barrel near the

Elberton's first Confederate memorial figure—Dutchy—was considered a Yankee by the townspeople. He was lynched by a drunken crowd and buried in the town square, where he stayed for decades. Courtesy of the Elberton Granite Museum.

site led some to claim Dutchy had gotten drunk and fallen off). The rabble buried "him" on the square, and a more conventional Confederate figure was created and placed on the pedestal. When Dutchy was exhumed in 1982, the red clay was removed by a run through a car wash, and the defamed monument found a home in the museum, where it is proudly displayed. *Elberton Granite Museum is on GA 17-GA 72 (College Avenue) in Elberton, P.O. Box 640, 1 Granite Plaza, Elberton, GA 30635 (706) 283-2551.*

An old, apparently forgotten Confederate cemetery can be found along the Bartram Trail just west of the Powerhouse visitors center at Clark Hill Dam, just off U.S. 221.

Petersburg

On May 3, 1865, Jefferson Davis and his entourage crossed the Savannah River on a pontoon bridge near Vienna, South Carolina, and landed at Petersburg, at the confluence of the Broad River. The community, Georgia's third largest in 1800, disappeared after the formation of Clarks Hill Lake. The site is occupied by Bobby Brown State Park, where a stone monument commemorates the frontier Fort James. *The park is twenty-one miles east of Elberton via GA 72, and south on Bobby Brown State Park Road.*

Lincolnton

In the center of town is a Confederate memorial, dedicated on April 26, 1924.

Chennault

Chennault House. Davis paused here on May 3, 1865, during his flight from Richmond en route to Washington, Georgia. On May 24 raiders attacked the gold train, seizing the remainder of the Richmond bank deposits, which some still believe to be buried nearby. Federals seized the treasury gold on June 4 in Washington. Union soldiers tortured family members in an attempt to discover other hidden treasures. *Northeast of Danburg at the junction of GA 44 and GA 79 in Lincoln County, fifteen miles from Washington.*

Washington

After fleeing Richmond when Lee abandoned Petersburg, Virginia, Davis stopped temporarily in Durham, North Carolina. When Johnston surrendered there to Sherman, Davis continued his flight through South Carolina into Georgia, stopping in Washington. His wife and children had passed through several days earlier. On May 5, 1865, Davis held the last cabinet meeting of the Confederacy in the Heard House, where he spent the night. With him were Braxton Bragg (his military adviser), C. E. Thornburg (a naval purchasing agent), I. M. St. John (commissary general), A. R. Lawton (quartermaster general), John H. Reagan (postmaster), and Burton Harrison (Davis's private secretary). The party split up to either return home or attempt an escape to Cuba, Mexico, or England. Davis traveled south with a small escort.

Robert A. Toombs House State Historic Site. Toombs was Washington's most famous and controversial citizen. He served in the Georgia legislature and the U.S. House and Senate but resigned from the latter in 1861. Toombs was prominent at the Montgomery

The magnificent home of Georgia's "unreconstructed rebel," Robert Toombs, is a state historic site in Washington.

convention, almost becoming president of the Confederacy; he settled for secretary of state. He later became a general in the Confederate army but resigned following the battle at Antietam, where he led a small group of Georgians in holding the famed Stone Bridge until Lee could bring up reinforcements. He returned to Georgia as adjutant and inspector general of the Georgia Militia at Atlanta and Savannah. When the Confederacy collapsed, Union troops entered Washington to arrest the fiery Toombs, whom they threatened to hang from an oak tree in front of his home, but Toombs escaped and made his way to Europe. After his return in 1867, he refused to take the oath of allegiance, dying in 1885 as the original "unreconstructed rebel." Toombs once stated, "I am not loyal to the government of the United States and do not wish to be suspected of loyalty."

His home (1791) has been restored as a state historic site and is listed on the National Register. It contains much of Toombs's furnishings, including the huge cast-iron chandeliers he brought from his home in Washington, D.C. Also featured are his papers and a film presentation of an "interview" with Toombs. *Robert Toombs House State Historic Site, 216 East Robert Toombs Avenue (U.S. 78), P.O. Box 605, Washington, GA 30673 (706) 678-2226.*

Washington-Wilkes Historical Museum. The first two floors of this interesting house (1835) contain elegant period furniture. The third floor houses an impressive Civil War museum with a notable Confederate gun collection, Joe Brown pikes, pistols, swords, pictures, documents, diaries, newspapers, a uniform that belonged to Robert Toombs, busts of prominent Georgians, and Jefferson Davis's camp chest, sent through the blockade by English admirers and presented to Col. John Weems by Col. Taylor Wood before the Davis party departed. Just inside the entrance to the house are two Civil War–era mortars. *308 East Robert Toombs Avenue (U.S. 78), Washington, GA 30673 (706) 678-2105.*

Mary Willis Library. In an alcove of this beautiful Victorian structure is one of Washington's most intriguing historic treasures: a massive cast-iron chest. When the Heard House was demolished in 1902, this enormous box was found in the basement. It was probably left by the Davis party and may have held part of the legendary lost treasure of the Confederacy. The original foot-long key has never been found. When the chest was opened in 1943 by a locksmith it was found to be empty. *At Liberty and Jefferson Streets, 204 East Liberty Street, Washington, GA 30673 (706) 678-7736.*

The present courthouse occupies the site of the Heard House, which was torn down early in this century. In front of the courthouse is a large stone that describes the last meeting of the Confederate cabinet and a Confederate statue dedicated on Confederate Memorial Day 1909.

Although her home, Haywood, no longer exists, Eliza Frances Andrews lived in Washington, where she wrote *Wartime Diary of a Georgia Girl.* It tells of her evacuation to south Georgia and her return amid the ruins of a Georgia devastated by Sherman's army. Especially interesting is her account of the Federal occupation and the return of Confederate veterans from Virginia and North Carolina. The book vividly conveys the hatred Southern women displayed toward their conquerors. Andrews became a highly regarded scientist and is buried in Resthaven Cemetery.

Edward Porter Alexander (1830–1910), West Point class of 1857, was a brigadier of artillery under Longstreet in the Army of Northern Virginia. His seventy-five massed guns bombarded the Union positions at Gettysburg prior to George Pickett's disastrous charge. Alexander fought in virtually every Virginia campaign and at Chickamauga. He is buried in Augusta. His home was the Gilbert-Alexander-Wright House on Alexander Drive.

The Ficklen-Lyndon-Johnson House (Holly Court, 301 South Alexander Avenue, 1825) was the refuge of Varina Davis for several days while she fled across the ruined Confederacy without her husband. The home is listed on the National Register. The Wickensham House (Robert Toombs Avenue) has the mantel from the Heard Building, and the Osborne-Bounds House (Spring Street) has its wrought-iron balcony. The David Toburen House (Alexander Street) is a wing from the Toombs House.

Washington was home to Louis Dugas, consulting surgeon of military hospitals, and John A. Campbell, who resigned his post as an associate justice of the U.S. Supreme Court in 1861 to become the Confederate assistant secretary of war. His home is the Campbell-Gordon House (East Liberty Street).

Robert A. Toombs (1810–85) rests beneath a draped obelisk in Resthaven Cemetery. Also here is Dudley M. DuBose (1834–83), a Confederate general who married Toombs's daughter Sallie.

Taliaferro County

Crawfordville

This is the site of the Alexander H. Stephens Home and Confederate Museum. Stephens was born into a poor family, but when his parents died, an uncle educated him in law. Stephens served in the state legislature and the U.S. House and became governor. Although he voted against Georgia's secession, the Montgomery convention selected him to be vice president of the Confederacy. A radical states' rights advocate, Stephens loudly opposed many of Jefferson Davis's policies, considering him to be a dictator, and spent most of his time during the war in Crawfordville. Arrested at home, he was reunited with Davis on his way to a six-month imprisonment at Fort Warren in Boston Harbor. The brilliant Stephens later wrote *A Constitutional View of the War Between the States,* giving the war its most popular name in the South.

Alexander Stephens, vice president of the Confederacy, is buried near his home, Liberty Hall, in Crawfordville.

Georgia acquired Stephens's home, Liberty Hall, from the U.S. government in 1933. Built in 1875 with materials from his earlier house, it is open to the public. A Confederate museum next door has an outstanding collection of Civil War military and personal artifacts and dioramas of combat and camp scenes. In front of the home is a sculpture of Stephens by Gutzon Borglum, who later abandoned the Stone Mountain project (*see pages 91–92*). Stephens is buried on the grounds beneath the Old Guard Tablet. First he had been buried in Atlanta's Oakland Cemetery at a funeral attended by twenty thousand people. Stephens's beloved brother Linton and his dog Rio are also buried here. *Two blocks north of the courthouse on Park Street; leave I-20 at exit 55; Alexander H. Stephens Home and Confederate Museum, P.O. Box 235, Crawfordville, GA 30631 (706) 456-2221.*

At the courthouse in town is an obelisk honoring Taliaferro County's Confederate dead, erected April 26, 1898. The speaker for the event, Gen. Clement Evans, requested and received a hearty Rebel Yell from the assembled veterans.

Robinson

A gun shop was established here to arm local Confederate recruits.

Raytown

Varina Davis spent the night of May 3, 1865, here, ironically at the ancestral home of Davis's parents and grandparents.

Warren County

Shoals

In November 1864 Federal cavalry covering Sherman's march destroyed mills in Shoals. There is a Confederate monument beside the courthouse in Warrenton.

Thomson

On the courthouse grounds is a joint McDuffie-Columbia County obelisk placed in 1896 to honor the men who served the Confederacy. Beside the railroad is a moving monument that pays homage "To Women of the Sixties." It features a female figure clad in homespun.

Appling

In the courtroom of historic Columbia County Courthouse (1810), behind the judge's bench, is a marble tablet listing the names of local men killed during the Civil War.

Gibson

A small park in front of the Glascock County Courthouse contains a plain obelisk erected to the memory of Calvin Logue, who donated twenty acres to establish the town in 1858. He was killed in August 1864 while leading his command at Deep Bottom, Virginia.

Augusta

This was the birthplace of Joseph Wheeler, Confederate lieutenant general and U.S. major general. Graduated from West Point in 1859, he rose quickly to the rank of general and commanded Confederate cavalry in the Army of Tennessee that opposed Sherman's campaign against Atlanta and the March to the Sea. He later served in the U.S. Army during the Spanish-American War and was buried at Arlington National Cemetery, the premier example of a reunited America.

Augusta housed a number of Confederate hospitals and refugees during the war. After his capture in south Georgia, Jefferson Davis was brought to Augusta and placed on a steamer, beginning his journey into captivity. Alexander Stephens joined Davis here. The community sent two thousand of its fifteen thousand residents to wage war.

When Sherman feinted on Augusta in November 1864, Confederate Gen. Braxton Bragg concentrated ten thousand men here and constructed ten earthen forts to protect the city. Cotton was piled six bales high on Broad Street, ready for barricades or burning.

Powder Works. Augusta became an important manufacturing center during the Civil War. On July 10, 1861, Jefferson Davis authorized Col. George Washington Rains to build a gunpowder factory for the Confederate government. After inspecting dozens of potential sites, Rains chose Augusta on the merits of its canal and abundant water power, railroad connections, and distance from the Union threat. Construction started in September and the project consumed five million bricks and granite from Stone Mountain. Rollers and equipment were gathered from Virginia, Tennessee, and other sites across the Confederacy. The works eventually extended for two miles along both sides of the Augusta Canal and occupied twenty-six buildings. It was the second largest such facility in the world, manufacturing 2.75 million pounds of gunpowder in three years of operation, 1862–65. Three million pounds of salt-

All that remains of Augusta's enormous gunpowder factory is this 176-foot chimney.

peter were consumed, much of it brought through the blockade from India but also taken from Georgia caves and old Southern outhouses. Rains boasted that the South never lost a battle for lack of powder. Also produced were cannon, cartridges, grenades, percussion caps, and signal rockets. Other facilities made pistols, gun and horse harnesses, uniforms, shoes, bedding, hospital supplies, dyes, and baked goods.

In 1872 Augusta purchased the complex from the federal government and demolished it for mills. Rains, then a local professor of chemistry and pharmacy, requested that the city spare the towering chimney "to remain forever as a fitting monument to the dead heroes who sleep on the unnumbered battlefields of the South." The Confederate Powder Works Chimney, 176 feet of brick, marks the site of the most important installation in the Confederacy, the only permanent structure started and completed by the nation. The surrounding Sibley Mill, with its crenelated parapets and battlements, resembles the Civil War works. *At 1717 Goodrich Street; the best view is from across the canal.*

The Augusta Confederate monument is one of the tallest and most expensive in the South.

In the 1700 block of Broad Street between Seventh and Eighth Streets is one of the most imposing Confederate monuments in the South. It was designed by Von Gunden and Young of Philadelphia and sponsored by the Ladies Memorial Association. The central shaft of the seventy-six-foot-tall monument was carved of Carrara marble in Italy. The base, made of Georgia granite, is surrounded by four life-sized figures of Lee, Jackson, and two Georgia generals who died in the war—Thomas R. R. Cobb and William H. T. Walker of Augusta. At the top of the shaft is a statue of a common infantryman to honor Augusta's volunteers. It was modeled after local veteran Barry Benson, a scout and sharpshooter who twice escaped from Union POW camps and whose memoirs are still in print. This memorial cost $17,332 and was dedicated on October 31, 1878, before a crowd of twenty thousand people. Clement Evans spoke, Stonewall Jackson's widow was present, but Alexander Stephens, although he was in town, could not attend because of inclement weather and his frail health.

Augusta-Richmond County Museum. In addition to other artifacts, the museum houses a collection of munitions that were manufactured in Augusta, dumped into the Savannah River at the end of the war, and later recovered. Its former location, the old Richmond Academy Building (540 Telfair Street, 1809), was used as a Confederate hospital after Chickamauga. Federals occupied the building until 1868. *560 Reynolds Street, Augusta, GA 30901 (706) 722-8454.*

Augusta Arsenal. In 1957 the warehouses and barracks of the U.S. Arsenal were converted into classrooms and other facilities to form the campus of Augusta College. The arsenal was established in 1793 by Pres. George Washington and maintained for 123 years. On January 21, 1861, an artillery battery, twenty thousand muskets, and abundant ammunition were stored here. Volunteers flocked from across Georgia and South Carolina to lay siege to the arsenal, whose eighty-man garrison surrendered to Georgia Militia Col. William H. T. Walker five days after Georgia's secession. The arsenal's captain, Arnold Elzey, then joined the Confederate army. The facility manufactured munitions for the Confederate armed forces throughout the war. People across the South donated all types of metal, including church bells, iron window weights, and bed frames for the manufacture of bullets. The largely female work force produced seventy-five thousand cartridges daily.

In a cemetery on the grounds is the grave of General Walker (1816–64), a native of Augusta who had risen to the rank of major general before being killed on July 22, 1864, at the head of his division at the opening of the battle of Atlanta. Walker, nicknamed "Shotpouch" for his propensity for being wounded (he was nearly fatally shot by Seminoles and then by Mexicans), had a terrible temper and resigned repeatedly from the U.S. and Confederate armies and the Georgia Militia for perceived slights. He might have challenged his superior, William J. Hardee, to a duel had he survived his final battle. Walker had advocated freeing and arming slaves for Confederate service. His remains were shipped via Millen in a roundabout journey during which his sword and scabbard were lost. A tall obelisk marks the grave. The cemetery grounds were part of his ancestral home. Walker's father, Freeman, had sold seventy acres for the arsenal, reserving the one-acre plot for a cemetery. A section of Confederate graves, men who died in the area hospitals, is beside the family plot. *2500 Walton Way, Augusta College, Augusta, GA 30904-2200 (706) 737-1444; (706) 823-6600.*

One of the earlier churches on the site of Saint Paul's Episcopal Church (1919; the fourth church on the site) provided a crypt beneath the altar for Leonidas Polk, the Confederate general killed

at Pine Mountain, but only for a century. After his body lay in state
for two days at the city hall, thousands followed his coffin to the
church for an elaborate funeral attended by a recuperating James
Longstreet. During the 1970s, the state of Louisiana, where Polk
had served as an Episcopal bishop for several decades before entering Confederate service, claimed the remains. *605 Reynolds Street,
Augusta, GA 30901 (706) 724-2485.*

First Presbyterian Church (1809). Designed by Robert Mills, who
was also responsible for the Washington Monument, this structure
and its grounds were used as a Confederate hospital and temporary
POW detention center. Woodrow Wilson's father, the ardent Secessionist Dr. Joseph R. Wilson, was pastor during the Civil War. As a
young boy, the future president saw Jefferson Davis being taken
through the town in chains. *632 Telfair Street, Augusta, GA 30901
(706) 823-2450.*

From 1858 to 1870 the Wilsons lived in the manse across from
the church. *Woodrow Wilson Boyhood Home, 419 Seventh Street,
Augusta, GA 30901 (706) 724-0436; administered by Historic
Augusta, Inc., 111 Tenth Street, Augusta, GA 30901 (706) 724-0436.*

The Medical College of Georgia was a Civil War military hospital. *598 Telfair Street, Augusta, GA 30901 (706) 721-7238.*

James Ryder Randall Monument. This statue made of Georgia
marble and erected in 1936 by the UDC honors the author of "Maryland, My Maryland," a popular Civil War song. Randall, a Balti-
more native, was teaching in Louisiana when Union troops subdued
Secessionist civilians in his hometown. Outraged, he wrote the poem
as an indictment of Lincoln. *At 1300 Green Street, between McKin-
nie and Canal Streets.*

Poet's Monument. This memorial, erected by the city in 1913,
honors several noted Georgia poets, including Randall (1839–1908),
Sidney Lanier (1842–89) of Macon, and Father Abram Ryan. Lanier
served as a Confederate soldier and died from tuberculosis contracted while in a Union POW camp. Father Ryan was the Confederacy's famed poet-priest. During the war Ryan served as an army
chaplain and afterward wrote a series of poems about the war that
were immensely popular in the South. His best-known work was

"The Conquered Banner"; others were "March of the Deathless Dead," "Land Without Ruins," and "The Sword of Robert Lee." *In a small park between McIntosh and Jackson Streets in the 700 block of Green Street.*

An obelisk to the Confederate dead from Saint James Methodist Church Sabbath School (439 Greene Street), dedicated in December 1873, stands in front of the church, which was famed for its large Sunday school. The monument, Augusta's first to the Confederacy, lists 24 members killed in the war and 290 other Augustans who died in service. The Church of the Most Holy Trinity (720 Telfair Street, completed in 1863) was a hospital after Union occupation. Arrival of the organ, ordered from the North, was delayed until the end of the war. The Victorian Confederate Widows Home (Second and Greene) has long since run out of widows.

Magnolia Cemetery. Here rest seven Confederate generals: Ambrose R. Wright, Victor J. B. Girardey, John K. Jackson, William D. Smith, Marcellus A. Stovall, Goode Bryan, and Edward Porter Alexander. Wright (1826–72) fought in Virginia and later owned the *Augusta Chronicle Sentinel.* Girardey (1837–64) was killed near Richmond. Jackson (1828–66) fought in the Army of Tennessee, where his brigade suffered 61 percent losses at Chickamauga. Smith (1825–62) of the West Point class of 1846 served at Secessionville, South Carolina, before dying of yellow fever in Charleston. Stovall (1818–95) served in the West from Perryville to Johnston's surrender in North Carolina. Bryan (1811–85) of the West Point class of 1834 fought with Longstreet in Virginia and at Chickamauga. Alexander was a brigadier of artillery under Longstreet in the Army of Northern Virginia and saw action in virtually every Virginia campaign and at Chicka- mauga. A monument surrounded by seven headstones, erected Jan- uary 15, 1994, by the Sons of Confederate Veterans, honors the generals buried here. James Ryder Randall is also buried here. One section of the cemetery contains the graves of three hundred Con- federate soldiers and sixteen Federal prisoners who died in hospi- tals, primarily in 1864. The section has a small pavilion for ceremonies. When Sherman threatened Augusta, the eastern wall of the cemetery was fortified; patches in the brick mark cannon

This memorial honors seven Confederate generals buried in Augusta's Magnolia Cemetery.

emplacements. *Magnolia Cemetery, 702 Third Street, Augusta, GA 30901 (706) 722-8688.*

Summerville Cemetery. Here is the grave of George Walker Crawford (1798–1872), a governor, secretary of war under Pres. Zachary Taylor, and president of Georgia's secession convention. Nearby is Charles Jones Jenkins Jr. (1805–83), a Georgia supreme court justice during the war who was elected governor in 1865. For defying military dictates and congressional Reconstruction laws, the military governor, Gen. George Meade, removed him from office on December 9, 1867, replacing him with Gen. Thomas H. Ruger, provisional governor. Jenkins responded by hiding the state seal, funds, and records until the next popularly elected governor, James Milton, took office in 1872. The General Assembly thanked Jenkins by presenting him with a gold replica of the seal. Gov. Alfred Cumming (1829–1910), West Point class of 1849, who served in Virginia, surrendered at Vicksburg, fought through Georgia, and was wounded on three separate occasions, is also interred here. *Johns Road off Walton Way in The Hill.* Jenkins's home was Green Court (2248 Cumming).

Montrose (2249 Walton Way) was the home of Col. Charles Colcock Jones Jr. (1831–93), mayor of Savannah when the war began and then chief of artillery for Georgia and South Carolina. He wrote a number of books about the Confederacy, including *The Siege of Savannah, The Dead Towns of Georgia,* and *Antiquities of the Southern Indians.*

A boulder memorial at Walton Way and Aumond Road marks the birthplace of Joseph Wheeler (1836–1900). Along the Augusta Canal on Fifteenth Street Northeast is a stone monument with a bronze plaque marking Jefferson Davis Avenue, dedicated in 1924 by the UDC. Rollersville Cemetery, at Hicks Street and Bohler Street, became a resting place for fallen Confederate soldiers during the war. *At U.S. 1 and GA 88 in Blythe is a Jefferson Davis Highway marker, placed by the UDC in 1930.* (There is no Civil War significance to the Jefferson Davis Highway markers; the route extends from Virginia to Texas and was laid out in this century to honor the former president.)

Twiggs Cemetery. Maj. Gen. David E. Twiggs (1790–1862), an elderly man generally credited with the loss of New Orleans in 1862, died three months later at the family plantation here. He had served in the War of 1812, various Indian wars, and the Mexican War. Twiggs was the second highest ranking general in the U.S. Army in 1861 before his resignation at Georgia's secession. *South of Augusta, at GA 56 and Goshen Industrial Boulevard.*

Fort Gordon. Although it is nearly inaccessible, Georgia's first Confederate monument, dedicated in June 1866, lies in Linwood Cemetery on the grounds of Fort Gordon. The small gray marker, placed by a Sunday school, reads, "Erected in Memory of Our Boys in Gray."

The U.S. Army Signal Corps Museum houses displays concerning military communications from 1860 to the present. Featured are Civil War wigwag flags, signaling torches and lanterns, and telegraph material. *Avenue of the States and Thirty-sixth Street, Building 36301, Fort Gordon, GA, 30905 (706) 791-2818.*

⋙5⋘

West Central
Georgia

THE WESTERN HALF of central Georgia made great contributions to the war effort, including food products from rural areas and cannon, rifles, munitions, uniforms, and dozens of other necessary articles from the factories and mills in Columbus and Macon. Many Confederate soldiers convalesced in temporary hospitals set up in schools, courthouses, churches, warehouses, and the homes of generous citizens, where they were lovingly tended by innumerable Southern women.

This area enjoyed a general peace until the final days of the war, when Union Gen. James Wilson raided through Alabama and Georgia a week after Lee's surrender.

LaGrange

Wounded soldiers were nursed by members of the Nancy Harts, a unique female volunteer militia organized in 1863. The women drilled and practiced shooting with all the antique firearms in town. When the Harts bravely marched out to meet Wilson's raiders on April 17, 1865, the Federals, ironically commanded by a Col. O. H. LaGrange, were charmed by their spirit, and bloodshed was averted. No property was damaged, and the Federals continued toward Macon.

Stonewall Cemetery. About three hundred soldiers are buried here who died while being tended in the area hospitals. Their graves are marked by marble headstones inscribed with name, company, regiment, and date of death. *103 Miller Street.*

Bellevue. Jefferson Davis and other Confederate notables visited this magnificent Greek Revival home, now a National Historic Landmark, which was built in 1854 by Benjamin Harvey Hill. Although Hill opposed secession, he became a member of the Confederate Senate and was a major supporter of Davis. Arrested at his home with Stephen Mallory, the Confederate secretary of the navy, Hill was soon paroled. While serving in the U.S. Senate, Hill played roles in the presidential election of Rutherford B. Hayes and in ending Reconstruction. In 1946 the Fuller E. Callaway Foundation presented the home to the LaGrange Woman's Club, which has preserved it. *204 Ben Hill Street, LaGrange, GA 30240 (706) 884-1832.* Hill's boyhood home is the John Hill House, seven miles southwest of LaGrange, on Cannonville Road off U.S. 19.

A Confederate monument dedicated on October 30, 1902, stands in front of the city cemetery on U.S. 29 east of downtown. L. M. Parks donated one hundred dollars to the monument provided it was placed prominently in the downtown area so "every pizen Yank" could see it. The Herndon-Glanton-Reeves House (524 Greenville Street) was used as a hospital by both sides. LaGrange Community Church (118 Church Street, 1846) was also a Civil War hospital. Mrs. Peter Heard, second in command of the Nancy Harts, lived at the Heard-Dallas House (206 Broad Street).

West Point

Because the railroads in Georgia and Alabama were of different gauges, cargo had to be transferred here between cars of the Atlanta and West Point and the West Point and Montgomery Railroads, which necessitated a large railroad yard. When the Union raiding party under Wilson left Montgomery in early April 1865, he split his forces to capture West Point and Columbus.

In 1864 Fort Tyler, a thirty-five-yard-square earthwork surrounded by a ditch, was positioned atop the highest hill west of the river to defend the Chattahoochee bridges and rail facilities. The parapet was made of five feet of packed clay, with a ditch ten feet deep and twelve feet wide in front. It was manned by 130 poorly equipped men, many of them being young or elderly civilians or convalescing soldiers from several local hospitals. They were commanded by Robert C. Tyler, a thrice-wounded veteran who fought this battle on crutches, having lost a leg in Tennessee. While stationed here as a Confederate quartermaster, he had designed and overseen the construction of the fort. The Federals under O. H. LaGrange had thirty-five hundred horsemen.

The initial Federal assault on April 16 was repulsed, but through the day the defenders' three cannon, a 32-pounder and two brass 12-pounders, were silenced, and a second attack inflicted heavy casualties. As the attackers climbed into the ditch, the desperate Rebels hurled lighted artillery shells at them. When Tyler was killed by a sharpshooter and hand-to-hand fighting erupted within the fort, the Confederates were surrendered by Col. James H. Fannin. Their losses were nineteen killed, twenty-eight wounded, and sixty-four prisoners. Others wandered away when the battle was over, and sixteen POWs were paroled to tend the wounded. The Federals destroyed 19 locomotives and 340 railroad cars loaded with supplies, then moved toward Macon. This was the last fort to be surrendered by the Confederacy.

Wilson set off the fort's magazine, which left a huge crater in the center of the small work. In 1895 the hole was expanded and the hilltop converted to serve as the city reservoir, but excavated dirt thrown on the southeastern portion of the earthworks preserved it.

The property was recently donated to the Fort Tyler Association, which cleared and paved a switchback trail up the steep slope and erected half a dozen simple but well-executed interpretive signs. The crater is fenced off, but there are plans to fill it in and reconstruct the fort. Dedicated on May 23, 1901, the Confederate monument was originally positioned east of the river. It has since been relocated here. *Sixth Avenue off Third via Tenth, on the hill; Fort Tyler Association, P.O. Box 715, West Point, GA 31833-0715.*

Pinewood Cemetery. Seventy-six Confederate and Federal soldiers are buried here, casualties of Fort Tyler and others who died while being tended in the area hospitals. Only nineteen are identified. Note the double grave of Tyler and his friend, Capt. C. Gonzales, also killed here. Tyler (1833–65) is largely a mystery, but it is known that he was with William Walker in Nicaragua and that he served in

Tennessee and Kentucky before losing his leg at Missionary Ridge. Tyler had been buried originally in the Reese family cemetery. *In Pinewood Cemetery on U.S. 29 in eastern West Point.*

On the western bank of the Chattahoochee, at the old Hawkes Library, is a boulder marking the spot where Winnie Davis, Jefferson Davis's daughter, delivered a speech. In introducing her, former Confederate Gen. John B. Gordon referred to "daughters of the Confederacy," a name that was soon adopted by women who wished to preserve the memory of the Lost Cause.

On May 29, 1893, the train bearing Jefferson Davis's body to Richmond (*see page 78*) stopped beneath a huge floral arch in West Point, where Gov. William J. Northern and his staff boarded as an honor guard. This was probably at the Freight Depot (1854) on U.S. 29 just across the Alabama line, which surprisingly escaped Wilson's destruction and may soon be restored. The Griggs House (204 North Eighteenth Street, 1858), in front of Fort Tyler, was a temporary hospital after the battle.

Hamilton

A Confederate monument dedicated to the memory of Confederate veterans from Harris County stands in front of the courthouse.

Columbus

This city was the Confederacy's third largest manufacturing center, exceeded only by Richmond and Atlanta. Many factories and mills turned out massive quantities of rifles, pistols, cannon, mortars, swords, ammunition, uniforms, shoes, tents, cloth, and flour. Of particular importance was the iron works, established in 1853 to fashion farm implements but used by the Confederacy to make iron plate, cannon, and engines for ironclads. The massive production facilities of Columbus kept the armies of the Confederacy supplied in the field. The city's manufacturing role required that it also be a major railroad and shipping center.

In February 1864, with casualties overflowing Dalton and Atlanta, a fifteen-hundred-bed hospital was established in eight buildings on Broad Street and in two saloons and the courthouse.

The citizens of Columbus first feared that they would be attacked from the east, expecting Sherman to advance toward Mobile after Atlanta fell, but by April 1865 they realized that any attack would come from the west, from Alabama. Columbus's military forces consisted of a few militia units, county reserves, factory workers, and men too young or too old for the regular army. They were commanded by Gen. Howell Cobb, who had barely completed a line of earthworks west of the Chattahoochee to protect the bridges when Wilson's troopers arrived late in the day on April 16 and immediately launched a rare night attack. The poorly trained militia put up a spirited defense, but their efforts were mostly wasted, having never been under fire before and shooting over the heads of the invaders. The defenders fled after the Federals breached the Confederate line and captured a bridge. The action, which occurred a week after Lee's surrender, is considered the last battle of the Civil War. Wilson destroyed 15 locomotives, 200 cars, 125,000 bales of cotton, 74 cannon, the iron works, quartermaster depots, and various paper, textile, and flour mills.

Local members of the Ladies Memorial Association decided to hold services for the Confederate dead on April 26, 1866, an appropriate date, they felt, for it was the first anniversary of Johnston's surrender to Sherman. After the association wrote to the newspapers across the South promoting the idea, most southern states adopted the date as Confederate Memorial Day.

Confederate Naval Museum. The historic *Virginia-Monitor* battle inspired Confederate hopes that ironclad warships could break the Federal blockade. In 1862 work began on the ironclad *Jackson* (locally called the *Muscogee*) in Columbus, which would be used to clear the Federals from the Apalachicola River. The 250-foot-long ship was powered by two propellers, each seven and one-half feet in diameter. It mounted six cannon on a gun deck protected by two feet of oak and four inches of iron plate and had a fifteen-foot-long iron-sheathed prow for ramming. Completion was delayed continually by lack of materials, and the ship was not finished when Columbus fell. Wilson admired the powerful ram, then had it burned and set adrift. The ship sank below the city.

An unarmored gunboat, the *Chattahoochee,* was built in 1862 down the river at Safford. The three-masted steamer, which was 130 feet long, 32 feet wide, and drew 10 feet of water, carried a crew of 111 and was armed with one 9-inch gun, one 32-pounder rifle, and four 32-pounders. In May 1863 the *Chattahoochee* sank when her boilers accidentally exploded. The ship was raised and repaired at Columbus, then set ablaze by Confederates when Wilson arrived. The *Chattahoochee* also sank downstream.

During the celebration of the Civil War centennial, the remains of both ships were raised and towed to Columbus for display at a unique facility, the Confederate Naval Museum. Parts of the hulls, including 180- and 30-foot sections of the *Jackson,* were placed on concrete mounts beneath a giant canopy. The museum displays artifacts recovered from the ships, such as cannon, engines, weapons, tools, and armor. Also on exhibit are fourteen models of Southern ironclads, displays concerning the Confederacy's naval history and technology, and a series of photographs illustrating how the ships were raised and transported to Columbus. Other exhibits chronicle the many ingenious inventions developed by the Confederacy in the fight against overwhelming Union naval superiority. These include torpedoes (now called mines), which destroyed a number of ships, and the first practical submarines.

The museum participates in a program that instructs volunteers about the Confederate navy. The docents dress like Southern sailors and demonstrate naval life for visitors. The museum may move to an enclosed site closer to downtown and the river. The salvaged ship hulls must be sprayed constantly for preservation, and an indoor, climate-controlled environment would be beneficial. *The Confederate Naval Museum is at U.S. 280 (Victory Drive) and Second Avenue, beside the city auditorium; 202 Fourth Street, P.O. Box 1022, Columbus, GA 31901-0102 (706) 327-9798.*

Linwood Cemetery. There are separate army and navy plots in the cemetery. In the naval section a mounted 6.4-inch rifled gun from the *Jackson* watches over the sailors killed by the explosion of the *Chattahoochee*'s boilers in northern Florida. In the Columbus Guards section are 125 graves, 13 unknown; the City Light Guards plot contains 79 graves, 15 unidentified. Some died in local hospitals, others in defense of the city. On March 10, 1865, residents began planning a monument to honor the local Confederates. The memorial, a wooden cenotaph, was erected in 1868. That year the Ladies Memorial Association defied the occupying Reconstruction government to hold a military burial for Gen. Paul J. Semmes.

More than eleven hundred Confederate soldiers are buried in private plots, including Gen. Henry L. Benning (1814–75), who led Hood's Corps in Virginia and earned the nickname "Old Rock." Fort Benning is named for him. Interments include the graves of John Dunlop, an English-born member of the *Virginia's* crew during her two days of glory at Hampton Roads, and Pleasant J. Phillips (1819–76), the Georgia Militia general responsible for the slaughter at Griswoldville. He attacked an entrenched Union brigade, losing 475 old men and youngsters. Gen. Paul Semmes (1815–63), first cousin to Confederate Adm. Raphael S. Semmes of the *Alabama,* was mortally wounded leading his brigade at Gettysburg. He had fought in every Virginia campaign up to that point and had lost three-fourths of his men at Antietam.

Another notable grave is that of Dr. Francis O. Ticknor, noted doctor and poet. In the military hospitals his family found a grievously wounded boy named Giffen. Although the doctors in attendance had given him no chance for survival, the Ticknors took Giffen to their home, Torch Hill, where he recovered and returned to his unit. Ticknor's poem "Little Giffen of Tennessee" was famous throughout the South. *On Linwood Boulevard between Seventh and Eighth Avenues.*

Riverdale Cemetery (100 Victory Drive) has another Confederate plot and a monument to the Confederate dead.

Columbus Iron Works Convention and Trade Center. The restored Columbus Iron Works (1853) now provides seventy-seven thousand square feet of impressive convention hall and display space. The old iron works produced cannon (including a breechloader fashioned from a ship's wheel shaft), weapons, munitions, and ship machinery. Power plants built at Columbus provided propulsion for more than a dozen Confederate ships. It was the second largest iron works in the Confederacy, behind only Richmond's famed Tredegar Iron Works. On the river is a historic steamboat landing where the *Jackson* was moored when Wilson destroyed the ship.

The Columbus Iron Works—which produced cannon, engines, and armor for Confederate ironclads—is now a convention center.

South Hall exhibits a variety of Columbus products. Of particular interest are two cannon. The Ladies Defender, made of brass donated by local women, was captured by Federal forces at Shiloh and displayed in Chicago and at Shiloh National Cemetery. In 1902 Congress ordered the cannon returned. The Red Jacket was a salute gun of the Columbus Guards, fired to celebrate each Southern state's secession, Jefferson Davis's inauguration, and Confederate victories. When Columbus was captured, the gun was thrown into the Chattahoochee. Found later and sold for junk in New York, it eventually found its way home. *Columbus Iron Works Convention and Trade Center (Columbus Convention and Visitors Bureau), 801 Front Street, between Eighth and Ninth, P.O. Box 2768, Columbus, GA 31902 (706) 322-1613; (706) 327-4522; (800) 999-1613.*

One Arsenal Place (901 Front Street) was part of the Columbus Iron Works. The W. C. Bradley Company (Front Avenue between Tenth and Twelfth Streets) was a warehouse district burned by Wilson and later rebuilt, as was Eagle Mill (1229 Front Street). The site of the Confederate Guards Armory is on First Street. The Guards fought in thirty-one battles; thirteen survivors of the unit surrendered at

Appomattox. Two mounted cannon are on the Chattahoochee Promenade between Eighth and Ninth Streets.

A draped obelisk honoring local Confederate veterans stands on Broadway, dedicated by Gov. Alfred Colquitt. Buried in the cornerstone is the flag of the Twelfth Georgia; seven men died carrying it at Antietam. A stone at Broadway and Fourteenth Street commemorates the final battle of the Civil War.

Fort Benning

The National Infantry Museum at Fort Benning has a large selection of Civil War artifacts, including cannon, rifles, flags, medical items, musical instruments, a field desk and bed, original hardtack, Confederate money, uniforms of both armies, a field surgical kit, a diorama of the battle of Columbus, many Confederate flags, a flag from the Federal Second Regiment of Colored Troops, and documents signed by Lincoln. One notable artifact is U. S. Grant's traveling liquor cabinet. The museum has recreated Gen. Henry L. Benning's parlor. Some of his personal papers preserved here reveal that it took him a month to walk home from Appomattox. *Five miles south of Columbus on U.S. 27, National Infantry Museum, Building 396 on Baltzell Avenue, Fort Benning, GA 31905 (706) 545-2958.*

Cusseta

In front of the library and beside the courthouse is a Confederate monument honoring the Confederate veterans of Chattahoochee County. It consists of a plaque set on a boulder.

Newnan

During his siege of Atlanta, Sherman sent Gen. Edward McCook's cavalry to destroy the Macon Railroad. Turned away from Griffin by the timely arrival of Joseph Wheeler's cavalry, McCook intended to move through Newnan—at that time crowded with refugees from the fighting to the north—cross the Chattahoochee, and return to Union lines. Wheeler, however, put McCook's rear guard to flight at

Line Creek, and the Federals entered Newnan on July 30, 1864, to find an unexpected contingent of Confederate troops bolstered by convalescents and boys. A volley caused the Federals to bolt, and McCook tried to make a stand at nearby Brown's Mill. The Confederates, outnumbered three to one, captured one thousand men, twelve hundred horses, and two guns and released five hundred Confederate prisoners.

A small stone slab honoring Wheeler's victory at Brown's Mill was placed at the intersection of Millard Farmer Road and Old Corinth Road, west of Newnan. Reenactments are held each July. *For information, call (770) 253-8874.*

Oak Hill Cemetery. During 1864 every train coming into this hospital center was packed with wounded men. More than ten thousand soldiers were cared for in seven field hospitals, including the Baptist and Presbyterian churches (the Methodist church was the only church used for services) and other buildings. The hospitals were supervised by Dr. Samuel H. Stout, medical director of the Department of Tennessee. Under the trees around the courthouse men rested in twelve-foot-by-one-hundred-foot sheds. Of 268 Confederate soldiers interred here, only two are unknown. In 1951 the federal government erected new marble headstones over the graves. A stone monument honoring the dead is in the cemetery. *Oak Hill Cemetery is on Bullsboro Drive.*

A Confederate monument dedicated in 1885 stands on the courthouse square. The twenty-two-foot-high memorial weighs thirty-two thousand pounds and cost two thousand dollars. Also on the grounds is a large memorial to William Thomas Overby, who was born in Coweta County. Captured in 1864 with five other men while serving in Virginia with John S. Mosby's famous rangers, all were hanged as guerrillas. Mosby retaliated in kind, and his men were afterward treated as prisoners of war. The former courthouse was struck by several Union cannonballs during the skirmish.

Male Academy Museum. The Coweta County Historical Society is restoring this structure, which houses Civil War artifacts, weapons, equipment, and a battle flag from Company I, Thirty-seventh Georgia, and occasionally features special Confederate exhibits. *30 Temple Avenue, P.O. Box 1001 (30264) Newnan, GA 30263 (770) 251-0207.*

Three red brick buildings on College Street, including College Temple (73 College), then a school for girls, were used as hospitals. Wheeler's headquarters was temporarily established at Buena Vista (87 LaGrange Street). The Virginia House (corner of East Washington and Jefferson, 1865) was a hotel that once had a second-story balcony from which Jefferson Davis spoke.

Grantville

During the war a local resident organized mule trains to transport precious salt from Panama City, Florida. His home, the Smith-Clover House (Smith Street), was a halfway station for soldiers returning from the surrendered armies. A 136-pound cannonball that fell from a passing train was placed by five sisters in the yard of the Smith-Wilson House (Griffin Street, 1864).

Liberty Hill

A public well in this tiny community survives; it was used in 1864 when Federal cavalry fleeing the disaster at Brown's Mill stopped for water. *West of GA 219 between Franklin and LaGrange.*

Glenn

Buried in the Mount Zion Methodist Church cemetery is Pleasance D. Wilson, a soldier in the Army of Northern Virginia and the blacksmith who shod Robert E. Lee's famed horse Traveller. Two miles west of Glenn, just off GA 109 near the intersection of CR 218 and CR 211, is the Adamson Cemetery where an unidentified Federal soldier is buried. He died on the trek from Brown's Mill. A poem relating his saga was carved on a concrete slab by N. B. Adamson in 1928. *Glenn is on GA 109 near the Alabama line.*

Talbottom

After capturing West Point, Wilson sent his cavalry racing east to seize Double Bridges, which spanned an island in the Flint River, so he could advance rapidly on Macon. Two regiments rode all night to surprise and rout fifty defenders at dawn, capturing five guns and the bridges intact. They then passed through Fairview and Pleasant Hill. At the courthouse in Talbottom is an obelisk, dedicated in 1904 to Confederate veterans.

Buena Vista

A Confederate memorial fountain was unveiled June 3, 1916, on the courthouse grounds.

Preston

The first Confederate flag in Georgia was displayed at the court-house on March 31, 1861, but the claim is disputed. Most of the population turned out to cheer as the standard was raised by a young woman, elected for the honor by the local militia. When the war ended, Federal occupation forces took a certain joy in chopping down the flagpole.

Fayetteville

Union cavalry passed through town in July 1864, destroying a train of five hundred wagons and seizing four hundred prisoners. The Fife House (1855) housed Fayetteville Academy, attended at one time by a student named Scarlett O'Hara. A Confederate monument dedi-cated on April 26, 1934, stands at the courthouse.

Griffin

Stonewall Cemetery. Five hundred Confederates and one Federal (Pvt. Nathan Kellogg of Illinois) are buried here. They were casual-ties of Atlanta and Jonesboro or died of disease in one of the many hospitals established here. Confederate Memorial Day services were held here on October 26, 1866, one of the earliest observances. Griffin is one of many claimants to having hosted the first.

A monument to honor the Confederate dead was erected in 1869, again one of the first in the South, and features an angel on a stone base with the inscribed command "Rest! Soldiers! Rest!" It had been ordered before the war for a family plot, but the Northern blockade delayed delivery. When it arrived the family could no longer afford the statue.

At the edge of the cemetery a boulder marks the site of Gen. Joseph Wheeler's headquarters during Sherman's occupation of Atlanta. A monument honoring Confederate women stands nearby. Just outside the cemetery, in Memorial Park on Taylor Street, is a Confederate memorial with a statue of a soldier on a stone shaft, placed in November 1909. *Stonewall Cemetery, on U.S. 41 (Taylor Street) in Griffin.*

Oak Hill Cemetery. John McIntosh Kell (1823–1900), a Confederate naval hero, is buried in Oak Hill Cemetery, across the highway from the Stonewall Cemetery. The ninety-fifth cadet to graduate from the Naval Academy, he spent his life at sea. Kell was the executive officer of the Rebel raider *Sumter* and served as executive officer of the famed *Alabama* and the ironclad *Richmond*. His grave slab has an anchor design, and someone has laid seven seashells atop it.

The Bailey-Tebault House (633 Meriwether Street, 1859) saw service during the war as a hospital and is now on the National Register.

The seashell-adorned grave of John McIntosh Kell, a renowned Confederate naval officer.

It is being restored by the Griffin Historical and Preservation Society. Most of the Georgians who fought in the Confederate army were mobilized in Griffin: cavalry at Camp Ector and infantry at Camp Stephens (the latter named for the Confederacy's Georgian vice president). Two miles north of Griffin on McIntosh Road a boulder marks the site of Camp Stephens, now surrounded on two sides by eroded earthworks.

Wilson's troopers burned Griffin's railroad facilities and warehouses in April 1865.

Thomaston

Glenwood Cemetery. Fifty-four soldiers are buried in the Confederate portion of the cemetery. They died in hospitals established in the courthouse, the Methodist and Baptist churches, a girls school, and warehouses. Dr. Edward A. Flewellen, a medical director of the Army of Tennessee, is buried here, too. *On Lee Street.*

A unique monument was erected in 1919 on the southeast corner of the Upson County Courthouse: a cannonball (purported to be the first shot hurled at Fort Sumter) mounted on a marble

A Thomaston native and witness to the bombardment of Fort Sumter retrieved the cannonball that started the Civil War.

base. It was retrieved by W. P. Alexander, a prominent Civil War–era correspondent and Upson County citizen, who presented it in 1861 to Mrs. Sallie White. Its claim to authenticity is as valid as any.

Also on the courthouse lawn is a Confederate statue unveiled in 1908 and a monument to John B. Gordon, who was born February 6, 1822, in Upson County.

Pettigrew-White-Stamp House (1833). The second oldest house in town was the home of W. P. Alexander, who sent a sketch of the new Confederate flag design from the Montgomery secession convention to Loula Kenda, who made one of the first flags in the South. The house is operated currently by the Upson Historical Society, and tours can be arranged. *800 South Church Street, Thomaston, GA 30286 (706) 647-0686.*

Bellwood (Logtown Road) was Loula Kenda's home.

Wilson's cavalry destroyed three factories and two trains here on April 19, 1865.

The Rock

This is the burial place of twelve unidentified soldiers who died in nearby hospitals. *On GA 36 between Thomaston and Barnesville; turn south on Rock Road beside The Rock Post Office.*

Taylor County

Near Reynolds is a farm where John B. Gordon lived the last twelve years of his life. A Confederate monument is on the courthouse lawn in Butler.

Macon County

Beside the courthouse in Oglethorpe is a marble block memorial to local Confederate veterans (1924). The bell of Oglethorpe United Methodist Church (Church and Randolph) was donated at the start of the war to the manufacture of cannon but was spared and returned after the war. It hangs in the 1892 belfry.

Robert Toombs bluffed his way past the Federal garrison at Montezuma as he escaped the country at war's end. In Montezuma a statue of a soldier stands guard in a park beside GA 49 north of town. Erected in the downtown area in 1911, the monument became a traffic hazard and was moved in the 1970s. There is no special cemetery for Confederate soldiers, but there are forty-four government headstones and fifty-two iron markers placed by the UDC in the Montezuma Cemetery to honor some of Macon County's many veterans.

Ellaville

A Confederate monument beside the courthouse was dedicated to Southern veterans in 1910. Confederate recruits drilled at old Bethel Camp Ground and at Quebec, six miles southwest of Ellaville.

Andersonville Prison

By early 1864 the Confederate government was trying to cope with tremendous numbers of Federal prisoners captured over the course of three years of war. Because most were housed in Richmond, a city under continuous attack, Southern officials searched for a more remote site, one far from the battle lines. They chose Andersonville because the climate was mild, water appeared plentiful, and it was well removed from the fighting.

A prison, the largest yet constructed in the Confederacy, was quickly built. It originally enclosed sixteen and one-half acres but was expanded to twenty-six acres. The enclosure—1,620 feet by 779 feet—was surrounded by a fifteen-foot-high stockade made of pine logs. A second stockade was later built around the first for additional security. Sentry boxes were erected at thirty-yard intervals, and prisoners who violated the so-called dead line—a four-foot-high fence rail erected nineteen feet from the wall—were shot. Eight earthworks studded with twelve canister-loaded cannon were built outside the walls to discourage mass escape attempts. The prison was secured by fourteen hundred Southern soldiers, mainly young and elderly.

Things went wrong from the beginning. Each day railroad cars delivered four hundred more men to Andersonville, also known as

Camp Sumter. Originally designed to accommodate ten thousand men, the prison housed forty-five thousand over a period of thirteen months, thirty-three thousand at one time. Each prisoner was allotted six feet of space. The water supply became polluted by waste, and the crippled Southern transportation system could not deliver sufficient supplies to sustain the men. Medicine, unavailable to Confederate casualties, was nonexistent. Prisoners died of disease—mainly smallpox and dysentery—malnutrition, scurvy, gangrene, and exposure. Nearly thirteen thousand died, one out of every four. The dead were buried shoulder to shoulder in trenches outside the prison walls.

In September 1864 most of the prisoners were transported to other facilities in eastern Georgia and South Carolina because of a rumor that Sherman planned to liberate the prison. Andersonville continued to operate on a smaller scale until the war ended.

Capt. Henry Wirz, commandant of Andersonville Prison, was arrested here by Wilson's cavalry in April 1865 and charged with conspiracy to murder Federal prisoners. The war was over, and the victors wanted revenge. The North had lost a quarter of a million men, and when the conflict seemed over, their leader was assassinated. Wirz was to be a scapegoat for the entire war. When he refused to implicate Jefferson Davis in the Andersonville tragedy, a military tribunal found Wirz guilty of thirteen murders and ordered him hanged on November 10, 1865, in Washington, D.C. He was the only war criminal of the Civil War.

Immediately efforts were begun to identify the dead at Andersonville and to mark the graves, work led by the renowned Clara Barton. In 1868 prisoners from Macon, Magnolia Springs, Thomasville, and other prisons were reinterred here. A search was initiated for Federal casualties throughout southern Georgia, mostly from Sherman's march, including those killed at Griswoldville and other skirmishes, those killed by sharpshooters, and those who died of illness and accidents. Bodies were exhumed from Covington, McDonough, Worthville, Eatonton, Milledgeville, Clinton, Irwinton, Sandersville, Davisboro, Louisville, Spier's Turnout, and Swainsboro. Many had been buried in unmarked graves, and some still rest there or in unrecorded graves in community cemeteries along the way. Only 460 of Andersonville's dead are unknown, and most of those were from battlefields and hospitals across Georgia, brought here for reburial.

The U.S. government purchased the property, and in 1879 the Women's Relief Corps, an auxiliary of the Grand Army of the Republic, purchased the prison site. In 1910 the land was given to the War Department and ultimately transferred to the National Park Service. The national cemetery, marked by long rows of headstones, is immaculately kept. The grounds are dotted with fifteen monuments erected by several states in memory of their dead sons. The first was donated by New Jersey in 1899. The last, a moving sculpture of three skeletal figures supporting each other, was placed by Georgia in 1976. Its inscription from Zechariah reads, "Turn ye to the stronghold, ye prisoners of hope." Other states represented are Connecticut, Illinois, Indiana, Iowa, Maine, Massachusetts, Michigan, Minnesota, New York, Ohio, Pennsylvania, Rhode Island, Wisconsin, and Tennessee (honoring her Unionist sons). The Sundial Monument commemorates Clara Barton's successful efforts to identify the dead, and another memorial contains Lincoln's Gettysburg Address.

The first man to die here was Adam Swarner—Section K, Grave 1; his brother Jacob is buried in Section J, Grave 4,005. The head-

Nearly thirteen thousand Union soldiers died at Andersonville and were buried in the adjacent national cemetery.

stone of L. T. Tuttle—Section H, Grave 2,196—is topped by a dove,
the only ornament found on any grave here. Andersonville's only
Medal of Honor winner rests in Section H, Grave 12,609; ironically
Sgt. James Wiley was awarded the decoration for capturing a Georgia regimental flag at Gettysburg. A number of African Americans
lie here, including one soldier from the famed Fifty-fourth Massachusetts Colored Infantry; their stones are marked CT for "Colored
Troops." The last prisoner, R. Hanson of Wisconsin, died in February 1865 and rests in Section H, Grave 12,848. John Rupert and
John Hines, killed accidentally by fellow Federal soldiers when Jefferson Davis was captured at Irwinville, are in Graves 13,696 and
13,697.

Of particular interest is the impressive rostrum where Memorial
Day ceremonies are held. At that time the park is festooned with
many large flags, and smaller flags are placed on each grave. Note
the six graves that are set apart from the others. These were the leaders of the gang known as the Raiders, prisoners who preyed on
weaker prisoners. They were arrested, tried, and hanged.

The prison site is adjacent to the cemetery, its wall outlined by
cement blocks. Here are additional monuments and iron fences
enclosing 27 wells and escape tunnels (there were 440 documented
escapes from 31 tunnels, some 120 feet long) dug by desperate prisoners. A beautiful structure has been erected over Providence
Spring, which appeared during a thunderstorm in answer to the prisoners' prayers for a fresh water supply. The earthworks, which contained cannon and enclosed various buildings, remain.

Archaeologists excavating part of the prison site discovered a
forty-two-inch section of the original stockade. That work cleared
the way for a two-hundred-foot-long reconstruction of the prison
wall. Included are several sentry posts, the dead line, and a variety
of shelters built by prisoners. Reenactors occasionally portray the
life of both prisoners and guards.

The park museum displays artifacts and a relief map of the
prison. A twelve-minute slide show describes the history of Andersonville Prison. The museum also maintains files on prisoners,
which are helpful for descendants of prisoners who frequently arrive
in search of a particular grave. A separate museum contains enlight-
ening, inspiring, and disturbing displays about American POWs

A portion of the stockade at Andersonville prison has been recreated.

from the Revolutionary War to the present. A new museum is being planned.

Andersonville is an active national cemetery. Joining the Civil War veterans are those who fought in the Indian wars, the Spanish-American War, World Wars I and II, Korea, and Vietnam. *Andersonville National Historic Site is between Oglethorpe and Americus on GA 49; Route 1, Box 800, Andersonville, GA 31711 (912) 924-0343.*

Andersonville Village

Just west of the prison, this was a quiet settlement when Confederate officials built the prison nearby and began marching prisoners through town to the stockade. An obelisk was erected in 1909 in the center of the town to the memory of Henry Wirz, considered a martyr by many southerners. Inscriptions on the shaft summarize the story of his conviction and execution in Washington, D.C., where he is buried.

The welcome center and museum (Box 6, Andersonville, GA 31711 [912] 924-2558) in the old train station houses a number of interesting Civil War exhibits, including a model of the prison. The Drummer Boy Museum (109 Church Street, Andersonville, GA 31711) offers a fascinating variety of displays relating to the common soldier, such as personal possessions, weapons, uniforms, and flags. Uniforms and drums of a nine-year-old Confederate and a thirteen-year-old Union drummer boy, the bonnet worn to the gallows by Mary Surratt (a conspirator in the Lincoln assassination), and the uniform of Johnny Clem (allegedly the youngest Union soldier in uniform) are on exhibit.

Adjacent to Andersonville is Confederate Village, a collection of rustic structures simulating the wartime village. Encampments and battle reenactments are held twice a year.

There is a walking tour of the town, which was a vital supply center long before it became the site of a prisoner

The Civil War's only convicted war criminal, Henry Wirz, is considered a scapegoat by many southerners. This monument in Andersonville Village defends his reputation.

of war camp. Some of the oldest surviving structures are an 1860 home that housed Confederates (four thousand were stationed in the area), Gen. John H. Winder's quarters at the Scott place (1850), and the post office (1860). Benjamin Dykes erected the post office and also leased the land to the Confederate government for the prison. The depot, Winder's headquarters, and the quartermaster storehouse are noted on the tour guide. *Civil War Village of Andersonville, 114 Church Street, Andersonville, GA 31711 (912) 924-2558.*

Two miles south on GA 49 is Trebor Plantation (1840), home of Robert Hodges, a Confederate chaplain who provided supplies and food for the prison. It featured prominently in MacKinlay Kantor's novel *Andersonville* (1955).

Americus

Oak Grove Cemetery. Conditions at nearby Andersonville Prison were so deplorable that Confederate guards also suffered a high mortality rate; 115 guards died and were buried at Andersonville. By 1880 the boundary wall at the prison cemetery had been moved and the Southern graves were being covered by forest. Funds raised by the Ladies Memorial Association for a monument was used instead to reinter the Confederates at Oak Grove Cemetery and mark the graves. Other Southern soldiers buried here were wounded during Jubal Early's famous 1864 raid on Washington, D.C., and died in the Bragg and Foard Hospitals. In August 1864, after a terrible explosion and fire killed some soldiers at the Foard, patients were moved to local homes. *At the end of Church Street near the Gate House in Oak Grove Cemetery.*

The Americus Confederate monument is in Rees Park at Taylor and Elm, south of downtown. Now missing its hands and rifle, the statue is somehow appropriate for the inscribed dedication: "For those who fought in their ragged old suits of gray." At the end of the war, Federal occupation headquarters were established on South Lee Street.

Barnesville

The Dixie Rangers, a local militia unit, clashed with Federal cavalry on April 18, 1865, on the edge of town.

Greenwood Cemetery. The cemetery holds the graves of 155 Confederate and 2 Union soldiers who died in the five hospitals established in the town during the war. Each grave is marked by a marble headstone. An obelisk was raised on the plot of ground in memory of the dead. *West side of town along the railroad tracks.*

A monument to the women of the Confederacy was erected in 1889 just east of the courthouse, now in a parking island. On the campus of Gordon College (established 1852), named for John B. Gordon, Confederate general and Georgia politician, are two Civil War cannon. The Pitts-Lambdin House (643 Greenwood Street) was headquarters for Confederate troops.

Milner

Milner Confederate Cemetery. Here 108 unknown men are buried who died in area hospitals, most from wounds suffered while defending Atlanta. Dr. John F. Hunt and other local people gave the men constant care. *On the Old Alabama Road near the intersection with Liberty Hill Road, one mile from Milner.*

Monroe County

Near Culloden on April 19, 1865, a local militia unit called the Worrill Grays, only two hundred strong, fought a two-hour action with Wilson's men before withdrawing. The clash was so brisk that two Federal soldiers who captured the Grays' flag received the Medal of Honor. Skirmishes were also fought at Society Hill and Montpelier Springs. Culloden has a Confederate museum on Main Street, which is open by appointment. Call (912) 994-9239; (912) 885-2249 (city hall).

Forsyth

Forsyth Cemetery. When Sherman started toward Atlanta, twenty thousand wounded and sick Confederates were transported here for care. The buildings of the Female College (Tift College) were used as hospitals. The original buildings later burned. Other hospitals, including the Hardee and Clayton, were housed in the courthouse, Lumpkin Hotel, stores, the Hilliard Institute, homes, and ten facilities in groves near the railroad. Following the battles around Atlanta, the townspeople would meet trainloads of casualties at the depot with food. This cemetery contains the graves of 299 unknown and 1 known soldier. A nurse, Honora Sweeny, who died while attending the men, is also buried here. The graves are marked by Vermont marble headstones inscribed "Confederate." Also interred here is Confederate Gen. Gilbert J. Wright (1825–95), a cavalryman in Virginia who returned home in November 1864 to recover from wounds and obtain mounts for the army. *In the city cemetery at the end of Newton Memorial Drive.*

The Conley Building on Adams Street is an 1848 stone freight depot where Confederate casualties were unloaded and which was a temporary hospital. There are plans to turn it into a museum with military displays. The nearby Forsyth-Monroe County Museum and Store (the 1899 depot) is on Tift College Drive. *P.O. Box 401, Forsyth, GA 31029 (912) 994-5070.*

A Confederate monument, designed by Frederick Hibbard and dedicated in 1908, stands on the courthouse lawn. Note that while most Confederate statues seem to be guarding their communities, this bronze memorial is marching on.

High Falls

High Falls State Park. This was a prosperous industrial town that supported a gristmill, a shoe factory, and a cotton gin until November 1864, when Joseph Wheeler burned the facilities as he retreated from Sherman toward Forsyth. The beautiful falls and later ruins remain. *Route 5, Box 202A, High Falls Road, Forsyth, GA 30233 (912) 994-5080.*

Macon

The city served as an important quartermaster center for the Confederacy, distributing supplies, ordnance, and munitions. Cannon, personal weapons, and ammunition were also manufactured. Because of the fighting around Atlanta in 1864, Macon became a large hospital and refugee center. When Milledgeville was captured in November, the state government was relocated to Macon, where the last session of Georgia's Confederate legislature met in 1865. Camp Wright, named for Gen. Marcus J. Wright, known for collecting Confederate military records, was established nearby in early 1864.

Union cavalry twice menaced Macon. In July 1864, Gen. George Stoneman's cavalry unlimbered their guns across the Ocmulgee River at the Dunlop Farm but were forced to abandon the attempt to capture Macon when Howell Cobb rallied militia units. In November of the same year Kilpatrick's cavalry feinted on Macon while Sherman passed to the east on the march to Savannah. His demonstration was also repulsed.

In April 1865, after Columbus fell, Cobb returned to Macon to form a defense, but news that Lee had surrendered and that Johnston and Sherman were observing a truce convinced Cobb to disband his force and surrender the city on April 20, although a few shots were fired on the outskirts of town. Wilson established his headquarters in the Lanier House (a now-demolished hotel), where Jefferson Davis and his family were briefly quartered after his capture near Irwinville. On February 1, 1879, while on a tour of military facilities in the South, Sherman stopped for dinner in Macon on his way from Atlanta to Savannah.

Rose Hill Cemetery. In the Confederate Square of the historic cemetery (1840) are the graves of six hundred Confederate soldiers and a few Federals. When the war ended, Mrs. Jane Lumsden Hardeman led an effort to gather all the soldiers who had died in the hospitals scattered across the county. A stone border surrounds the enclosure, and simple stones lie in rows along the hillside.

Rose Hill also holds three Confederate generals: Edward Dorr Tracy, Alfred Holt Colquitt, and Philip Cook. Tracy (1833–63) was a native of Macon. He was at the head of an Alabama unit when he was killed at Port Gibson, Mississippi. Colquitt (1824–94) was a governor of Georgia and a U.S. representative and senator. He served in Virginia and at Olustee, Florida. Colquitt led the famed Colquitt's Brigade, which desperately defended South Mountain in September 1862 in Maryland, giving Lee time to organize his forces at Antietam. Cook (1819–98) rose through the ranks from sergeant to brigadier in Virginia. After the war he supervised the construction of the capitol in Atlanta. Also buried here is Peter J. Bracken, the engineer of the locomotive *Texas,* who aided in the apprehension of the *General* in the Great Locomotive Chase. In 1971 a monument of Georgia marble engraved with a likeness of the *Texas* was placed on his grave. A new historical marker honors Col. John B. Lamar, mortally wounded at South Mountain; he was a personal aide to Howell Cobb, his brother-in-law. *Rose Hill Cemetery, 1071 Riverside Drive, Macon, GA 31201 (912) 751-9119.*

Riverside Cemetery. Several blocks north of Rose Hill, on Riverside Drive, is a remarkably preserved artillery battery, part of the line that twice repulsed Federal attackers. Within the earthwork is the grave of famed boxer "Young" Stripling.

Dunlop Farm. During their raids against Macon, the Federals tore down stables and built temporary breastworks with the timbers. Twice the militia held them off. A large artillery position can be seen on the grounds of Ocmulgee National Monument, an archaeological site. *Ocmulgee National Monument, 1207 Emery Highway, Macon, GA 31201 (912) 752-8257.*

Old Cannonball House and Confederate Museum. The two brief attacks against Macon produced only one tiny act of destruction. During the July raid a single cannonball hit the sidewalk in front of Judge Asa Holt's home, pierced a column, and bounced into the parlor. The Cannonball House, an elegant 1853 Greek Revival structure, has been restored to a Civil War setting. The chairs in the dining room have been upholstered with needlepoint copies of southern state seals used during the war. Behind the house, in the old servants quarters, is a Confederate museum where the prized artifact is Mrs. Robert E. Lee's rolling pin. Recently placed on the grounds is No. 41, a 12-pounder bronze Napoleon cannon cast at the Confederate States Armory, site today of the Department of Family and Children's Services. The bells from Mulberry Street Methodist Church, Christ Church Episcopal, First Presbyterian, and First Baptist were donated to the armory. *856 Mulberry Street, Macon, GA 31201 (912) 745-5982.*

Sidney Lanier House (1840). Lanier, one of the South's great poets, was born in Macon in 1842. After volunteering for the Confederate army, he was captured on a blockade-runner. While he was held in a Federal prison, he contracted a lung disease that shortened his life. His home is maintained as a museum. In the Washington Street Library is a bust of Lanier by Gutzon Borglum. Lanier's law office, shared with his father and an uncle, was at 336 Second Street. The uncle, Clifford Anderson, a Confederate congressman and Georgia's attorney general, lived at 642 Orange Street (1859). *935 High Street, P.O. Box 13358 (31208), Macon, GA 31201 (912) 743-3851.*

First Presbyterian Church. Several versions of a familiar story are told. At Thanksgiving during the Union occupation in 1865, General Wilson ordered the U.S. flag flown from the entrance to the sanctuary. The pastor refused to participate and was replaced by the Reverend Francis R. Goulding, whose entire service consisted of reading from Psalm 131: "For they that carried us away captive required of us a song." The congregation then departed by the back door to avoid the Stars and Stripes. *690 Mulberry Street.*

Christ Church Episcopal. The original bell was melted down for arms in 1863, and the present one, donated in 1868 by A. A. Rolf, is inscribed, "On earth, peace, good will to men." In 1867 Sidney Lanier married Mary Day of Macon here. *538 Walnut Street.*

East Macon Methodist Church (1870). The congregation had just renovated an old school building when it was burned by Union soldiers, who used the pulpit as a horse trough. *424 Church Street.*

Bibb County's Confederate memorial, an Italian marble statue on a base of Georgia granite, stands in front of the Hart Building at Second Street and Cotton Avenue. Gov. Alfred H. Colquitt spoke to a crowd of forty thousand, twice the city's population in 1879. Atop the thirty-seven-foot base is the tallest statue in Georgia: ten feet six inches. A monument honoring the women of the Confederacy was dedicated on June 3, 1911—Jefferson Davis's birthday—at Poplar and First. On one side figures depict a woman tending a wounded soldier; on the opposite side she cares for a child. A carving on the monument illustrates a normal home setting, and a second scene reveals a

A Southern woman ministering to a wounded soldier is depicted on one side of Macon's monument to the women of the Confederacy.

home ravaged by war. Downtown, atop Coleman Hill, now occupied by the Walter F. George School of Law of Mercer University, a new stone monument has been erected on the site of the Marshall Mansion, where in 1887 Jefferson Davis delivered a speech and reviewed Confederate veterans.

The city hall (Poplar and First, 1832) was used as a Confederate hospital and served as Georgia's Civil War capitol between November 18, 1864, and March 11, 1865, when Joseph Brown convened the last meeting of the state legislature in the Confederacy. The Volunteer's Armory (480 First Street), opposite the Women of the Confederacy monument, has busts of Lee and Jackson over the entrance.

The Hay House (934 Georgia Avenue, Macon, GA 31201 [912] 742-8155), completed a year before the Civil War began, was the alleged hiding place of the Confederate or Georgia treasury. Although the tale is undoubtedly bogus, a secret room is featured on a tour of the mansion, one of America's finest. It supposedly led to a tunnel. The story originated when William B. Johnston, a Confederate treasury official, brought records here from endangered Richmond. He resided at the Johnston House at Georgia Avenue and Spring Street.

The Baber House (577 Walnut, 1830) was the headquarters of Maj. Gen. Howell Cobb, commander of the Georgia Militia and Reserves during 1864 and 1865 when the state government met here. James M. Green, surgeon general of Macon's Confederate hospitals, lived at the Green-Poe House (841 Poplar Street, 1840). The Edward Dorr Tracey House (974 Magnolia Lane, 1830) was the home of the general killed at Port Hudson, Mississippi.

Union Gen. James Wilson occupied the Woodruff House (988 Bond Street [912] 744-2715, 1836) during Macon's occupation; his staff camped in a tent city on the grounds. The Jefferson Davis family visited Macon in 1887 and received many tributes, including being guests of honor at a ball hosted here. The house is now owned by Mercer University and open by appointment. In Central City Park is a bandstand from which Davis spoke, and the Hill-O'Neal Cottage (535 College Street, 1856) has iron railings from the balcony of the Old Union Depot, another scene from which Jefferson Davis gave a speech.

The old Railroad District—south of the restored train depot on the railroad below Seventh Street and bordered by Seventh, Pine, and Hawthorne Streets and a swamp, which is now the Brosnan Yards of the Southern Railroad—was the site of Camp Oglethorpe, a drilling-parade ground for local militia and a fairground before the war. During the war it came to be used as a prison for Union officers; Andersonville held only enlisted personnel. Up to fourteen hundred men were held here at one time in a three-acre area enclosed by a twelve-foot-high board fence and guarded by sentries spaced every ten feet and by four 12-pounder guns. When the prison camp was threatened to be liberated by Union cavalry in July 1864, twelve hundred men were sent to Savannah and Charleston. Gen. George Stoneman was taken prisoner in the action and was briefly held here. The dead were reburied at Andersonville.

Fort Valley

Oak Lawn Cemetery. Twenty unknown soldiers are buried here. They died in a train wreck three miles north or in the local military hospitals: Buckern, Gamble, and several temporary facilities. Also buried here is Charles D. Anderson (1827–1901), a prewar mayor. He served in every Virginia campaign from the Peninsula to Chancellorsville; Anderson was wounded and captured at Antietam, then exchanged. Returning to Georgia in 1864, he led Georgia guard units around Atlanta and against Sherman's March to the Sea, where he suffered heavy losses at Griswoldville. *In Oak Lawn Cemetery on GA 49 south of town.*

Houston County

After the capture of Jefferson Davis, his guards camped at Bonaire on the way to Macon. Thaddeus Oliver is buried in southern Houston County; he wrote the famous Civil War poem "All Quiet Along the Potomac Tonight." Born in nearby Twiggs County, Oliver served in the Army of Tennessee and died of his wounds in 1863 in a Charleston hospital. A Confederate monument has stood at the courthouse in Perry since June 1907. An earlier memorial, a wooden shaft, stood in Evergreen Cemetery.

Vienna

The distinguishing feature of the Confederate monument in the town square in front of the courthouse is the statue's kepi. The memorial was unveiled in November 1908.

Cordele

The Suwanee Hotel on Eleventh Avenue (recently burned) was the site of Joe Brown's home and is said to have been Georgia's capitol during the last days of the war. Crisp County's Confederate monument was erected in a park at the corner of East Sixteenth Avenue and South Seventh Street.

Georgia Veterans Memorial State Park. This facility salutes all Georgians who have served in the armed forces since the Revolutionary War. In the museum-park headquarters is a display of a cannon and caisson, a sword case, and photographs in honor of the 125,000 Georgians who served the Confederacy. *Nine miles west of Cordele on U.S. 28; 2459-A U.S. 80 West, Cordele, GA 31015 (912) 276-2371.*

Cochran

Although this memorial was erected in the county seat of Bleckley County, the Confederate statue honors Pulaski County veterans. When it was dedicated in 1910, Cochran was a part of Pulaski. *Downtown in front of the school beside the courthouse on GA U.S. 23-GA 87.*

Hawkinsville

The Confederate monument at the courthouse was dedicated on July 31, 1907. Beneath the soldier are figures of Lee and Jackson. Stonewall lost his left arm to an automobile in 1937, which is the same one he lost at Chancellorsville, complications from which caused his death. Taylor Hall (1824), on the National Register, built across the Ocmulgee in Hartford by Robert N. Taylor and rebuilt on Kibee Street in 1836, hosted Federal troops at the end of the war.

Eastman

A Confederate monument stands on the courthouse grounds. It was unveiled on Confederate Memorial Day 1910. Jefferson Davis camped the night of May 7, 1865, three miles southeast of Eastman. A small monument marks the site off U.S. 23 on CR 265 near its intersection with CR 251. Davis's carriage driver was present in 1918 at the dedication.

Abbeville

After passing through Dodge County, Jefferson Davis traveled by swampy roads and crossed the Ocmulgee River at Poor Robin Ferry near Abbeville, camping here the night of May 8, the day before his capture. CR 224, north of the intersection of GA 30 and U.S. 129-GA 11, leads to the site. The campsite is marked by a large boulder on the courthouse lawn, dedicated by the UDC on June 3, 1925. A statue of a Confederate soldier was erected across from the courthouse and dedicated on April 26, 1909.

6

The March to the Sea

DURING WILLIAM TECUMSEH SHERMAN'S march from Atlanta to Savannah, the eastern central portion of Georgia witnessed what has been called the first modern display of total warfare: the destruction, not only of military targets, but also of the civilian economic system that undergirded the military structure.

After capturing Atlanta, Sherman evicted all civilians from the city and rested his army. John B. Hood decided to strike north, certain that he could draw the Federals out of the city and destroy them in the field. Sherman chased the Confederates into northern Alabama, but Hood refused to give battle. Returning to Atlanta in early November 1864, Sherman proposed an aggressive new strategy. He sent half his men to Tennessee to protect Nashville from Hood but kept fifty-five thousand infantry, five thousand cavalry, sixty-five cannon, and three thousand wagons as a force to advance against Savannah, which he would then use as a staging base to invade the Carolinas.

Sherman divided this army into two wings. The Army of the Tennessee comprised the right wing and executed a feint on Macon; two corps of the Army of the Cumberland—known as the Army of Georgia—made up the left wing and advanced on a parallel path forty miles to the east and performed a feint on Augusta. Since Hood had departed with the Army of Tennessee, there would be no significant military opposition, only harassment by Confederate cavalry under Joseph Wheeler.

Intending to destroy military and government property in Atlanta, Sherman allowed his men to run amuck in the city. As a result, the entire city was virtually destroyed. Only four hundred of thirty-six hundred structures remained. The Union army left a smoking ruin on November 15 and occupied Savannah a little over a month later on December 21. With no appreciable losses, Sherman's troops caused an estimated $100 million worth of destruction, four-fifths of it wanton by his own estimate. The Federals destroyed two hundred miles of railroad track and stole or slaughtered sixty thousand horses and mules. True to his boast, Sherman had made Georgia howl. It took decades for the state to recover.

Conyers

This was Sherman's headquarters as the left wing camped around Rockdale County on November 17, 1864, having destroyed the railroad from Lithonia to the Yellow River. On May 9, 1865, Wheeler was arrested here, paroled in Athens, then rearrested and sent north with Jefferson Davis. He was released from Fort Delaware on June 8. Conyers was the home of Joseph T. Albert, who was mortally wounded in Virginia at Second Manassas. He died before his wife arrived to care for him, but she had the body packed in a barrel of salt and brought home for burial. A rededication of the grave in 1962 featured Gov. Marvin Griffin.

A Confederate monument downtown was erected in 1913.

Henry County

Sherman's right wing, under Oliver O. Howard, left Atlanta via the McDonough Road and passed through Stockbridge and McDonough on November 15–16. Skirmishes between Federal cavalry under Judson Kilpatrick and Confederate cavalry commanded by Alfred Iverson occurred on the edges of the march, particularly at the Cotton River, defended by the now-mounted Orphan Brigade. Federals burned two churches, slaughtered animals in a third, and destroyed gristmills at Peachtree Shoals on the South River.

On the courthouse grounds in McDonough is a Confederate monument, dedicated on April 26, 1911, and a Confederate drinking fountain, placed in 1915. In the city cemetery, on Cemetery Street off Macon Street from the square, is the grave of Gen. Charles T. Zachary, wounded four times in Virginia before helping save Florida at Olustee. Shingle Roof Camp-ground, north of McDonough, was a mobilization point for local troops. According to legend, Oaklea Manor (1860), on Wynee Road near Hampton, was a Union headquarters during the march and was spared burning because the owner was a Mason.

Covington

On June 21, 1864, Federal Gen. Kenner Garrard led a cavalry raid that destroyed a newly constructed hospital center of thirty buildings, four wagon bridges and two rail-road bridges over the Yellow and Alcovy Rivers, and six miles of track between the Alcovy and Lithonia. This action disrupted

A unique Confederate monument—McDonough's water fountain.

transportation between Atlanta and Augusta and guaranteed that Hood would not be reinforced from Virginia or the Carolinas. Gar-rard burned the depot, two thousand bales of cotton, large amounts of government supplies, and trains. Sherman and the left wing camped in the area November 17–18 and crossed the rivers by pon-toon bridges.

Southview Cemetery. More than twenty thousand sick or wounded soldiers from the Atlanta area were treated in Covington's Confed-erate hospitals. Many of the men who died were reinterred near their homes after the war, but the graves of sixty-seven known and eight unknown men remain. Two Southern generals, Robert J. Henderson and James P. Simms, rest here, too. Henderson (1822–91) fought in the western campaigns, including Atlanta, and returned home to find Sherman had destroyed his farm and mills. Simms (1837–87) was in Virginia until captured at Sayler's Creek on April 6, 1865. *Southview Cemetery, at the end of Davis Street.*

A Confederate monument was unveiled on April 26, 1906, at the courthouse. Symbolically facing the setting sun, the statue honors the men and women of the Confederacy.

Four Confederate generals came from Newton County, including Henderson (the 1828 Swanscombe at 1164 Floyd Street Northeast, was owned by him) and Simms (the 1850 Graham-Simms House across the street at 1155 Floyd Street Northeast was his home). Damaged during the war, the Georgia Railroad Depot (4122 Emory Street Northwest, 1855) was repaired in 1868 and is now a restaurant. The First United Methodist Church (113 Conyers Street Southeast, 1854) had its pews removed when it was converted to a hospital. Sherman camped outside town on November 18 on the plantation of John Harris, at GA 64 and U.S. 278. Confederate soldiers hid in the chimney of the Clairmont mansion while he passed through.

Still standing west of Covington, on Jeff Cook Road just off GA 142 on the route to Newborn, is the Burge Plantation, home of Dolly Sumner Lunt. From an abolitionist family in Maine, she came to Georgia to teach and married a wealthy landowner who died prior to the war. In her famous diary, *A Woman's War-Time Journal,* she vividly described the looting carried out on November 19 by one of Sherman's passing divisions.

Oxford

On Asbury Street is the Zora Fair Cottage (1840), where young Zora reportedly hid after an unlikely spying adventure within Sherman's lines at Atlanta while disguised as a mulatto. Captured after pickets fired on her, she overheard conversations at headquarters and managed to escape. What appears to be true is that Sherman read of the supposed exploit in letters intercepted here and attempted to seize the girl to "scare her." She could not be found and died a few months later in South Carolina. The Oxford Cemetery (1839) on Emory Street has a section where a number of Federal soldiers are thought to be buried.

Bishop James O. Andrew, who served the local Methodist church, inherited a slave named Kitty. The church did not allow ministers to own slaves, but Georgia did not allow the freeing of slaves, so Andrews built the woman her own home, which is preserved at Salem Campground near Conyers. This incident led to the 1845 split between the northern and southern branches of the Methodist Church. Kitty is buried in the Oxford Cemetery.

Oxford Confederate Cemetery. While Oxford College closed for the duration, Few and Phi Gamma Halls were used as hospitals during 1864, and the thirty-one soldiers from Georgia, Alabama, Mississippi, Tennessee, Louisiana, and Florida who died there are interred in this quiet soldiers cemetery. Five of them are unknown. An obelisk to their memory was erected in May 1872. *On the Nature Trail 150 yards behind the Williams Gymnasium.*

Oxford and Oxford College of Emory University are north of Covington on Emory Street (GA 81).

Shady Dale

South of Covington on GA 83, this community was a large plantation visited by Sherman. An old well and monument memorializes a famed stagecoach hotel on the Augusta-Milledgeville-Macon route. Legend has Sherman spending a night here. It burned in 1868.

Butts County

Sherman's right wing camped around Jackson, Indian Springs, Iron Springs, Flovilla, and Cork on November 17–18 while securing a passage over the Ocmulgee River at Planters Ferry (Seven Islands). The site is in a rural area reached by primitive roads. Federals slaughtered hundreds of weakened horses on an island there, their bones remaining for decades. Local tales claim that the people of Jenkinsburg were so destitute they attacked and pillaged a Union supply wagon train. The county suffered a million dollars' worth of property damage.

The Confederate monument at the courthouse in Jackson was unveiled on April 26, 1911. On the courthouse square only the Masonic hall survived Sherman's visit.

Union troops camped at Indian Springs, which features beautiful shoals and natural spring water that has been coveted for centuries. The restored Indian Springs Hotel (1823) was built by Creek Indian chief William McIntosh. *Indian Springs State Park, Route 1, Box 439, Jackson, GA 30216 (770) 775-7241; Historic Indian Spring Hotel, GA 42, Jackson, GA 30216 (770) 775-6734.*

Madison

The students at two female colleges cared for Confederate casualties in hospitals and made clothing and blankets for them from carpets. This city was visited in July 1864 by Col. Silas Adams's retreating Federal cavalry, which burned Confederate stores. On November 19 Sherman's men destroyed railroad facilities at Buckhead, where they camped, and set up a temporary hospital in Rutledge. Ferry boats, gins, mills, and presses along the Oconee River were burned. In Madison, the Federals looted the business district and torched cotton, Confederate supplies, a slave pen, and railroad property. The depot, believed to be the first brick railroad station in Georgia, was partially burned by the Federals and is now a warehouse on West Jefferson Street. Andrews's raiders were imprisoned here for three days when Chattanooga was threatened.

The Morgan County Historical Society has its headquarters at Heritage Hall (1842). It offers a slide-show tour of many antebellum homes and sponsors Christmas tours. A Confederate and a Federal sword are on display. *277 South Main Street, P.O. Box 207, Madison, GA 30650 (706) 342-1612; (706) 342-9627.*

Madison Cemetery. Buried here are one known and fifty-two unknown Confederate soldiers and one black attendant who died in local hospitals. Note that there are two Confederate plots, one on either side of the railroad tracks.

Also buried here is Joshua Hill, a U.S. senator who opposed secession but resigned when Georgia left the Union. After his son, Legare, was killed on May 19, 1864, while fighting in the Confederate rear guard at Cassville, friends dragged his body into a house and pinned his name to his coat. Kind Federals marked his grave. En route to retrieve the body, Hill journeyed to Atlanta and introduced himself to Sherman as a friend of his brother, U.S. Sen. John Sherman. The Federal commander served Hill supper with political conversation, then issued him an escort and an ambulance to complete his mission. As Sherman's left wing approached Madison, Hill met the Union column and asked protection for the city. Contrary to popular legend, Sherman did not find the city "too beautiful to burn." He passed to the west of Madison with the Fourteenth Corps. Civic leaders can be forgiven for the exaggeration—the small town has thirty-five houses on the National Register that can be viewed during a walking tour. *In the city cemetery west of U.S. 129 on Central.*

Presbyterian Church (1842). Federals stole the beautiful communion service from this stately church, but when citizens complained, it was returned by order of Gen. Henry W. Slocum. *382 South Main Street.*

Madison-Morgan Cultural Center. Established in an elegant 1895 brick school building, the museum has an original log cabin reconstruction and features Civil War exhibits, including the Presbyterian communion service (referred to above) and a quilt on which a wounded veteran drew a battle scene from Virginia (his wife later embroidered it). *434 South Main Street, Madison, GA 30650 (706) 342-4743.*

The Carter-Newton House (530 Academy Street, 1849) was the site of the Madison Male Academy, where young Alexander Stephens taught. Barrow House (420 Porter Street, 1840) was a Civil War hospital. The Judge A. H. Winter House (258 Academy Road) was home to the last surviving Confederate veteran in the country. Renovation of the Magnolias (South Main Street, 1860) revealed a trap door leading to a tunnel, presumably a stop on the Underground Railroad.

The Confederate monument in a park near the cultural center on Main Street was dedicated on April 26, 1908. A Jefferson Davis Highway marker is on Main just south of the business district.

Jefferson Davis spent a night at Park's Mill (1806), on the Oconee River, while being pursued by Federal cavalry. In 1981 the house was moved from the original site of the home, ferry, and mills because of the creation of Lake Oconee. The Cousins family of Robins Nest Farm (2440 Bethany Road, the Old Eatonton Road), a beautiful plantation home, was neutral, having relatives fighting on both sides of the conflict. Gen. Henry W. Slocum's column camped on the grounds. Hickory Hill Farm (6080 Bethany Road, 1830) in Buckhead was a Union hospital following a nearby skirmish in July 1864. Four months later Sherman's men camped here. Union cavalry spent a night under the great oaks at the Ardenlea Farm (2900 Dixie Highway, 1820). Union Capt. James H. Ainslie of Ohio later purchased the place and is buried on the grounds. The Hill-Baldwin-Turnell House (485 Old Post Road, pre-1840) was the postwar home of Joshua Hill. Although Hill opposed secession, his sons fought for the Cause and his daughter married a Confederate soldier.

Jasper County

George Stoneman's cavalry passed through the county in July 1864. During November 19–20 Sherman's right wing crossed the Ocmulgee River at Planter's Ferry on two pontoon bridges. Half of the line marched through Monticello, while the other portion moved directly to Hillsboro over roads no longer in existence. An obelisk, erected to honor Jasper County's Confederate veterans, was erected in 1910 at the courthouse square. Benjamin Harvey Hill, a U.S. congressman before and after the war, was born near Hillsboro, where a stone monument honors him. He opposed secession but became a prominent Confederate senator, generally supporting Jefferson Davis and greatly helping the president's relationship with Georgia's highly independently minded Gov. Joseph Brown. After the war he returned to the U.S. Senate and played an instrumental role in the end of Reconstruction and the removal of federal troops from the South. A Union soldier who died on the March to the Sea is buried in the Baptist church cemetery.

Putnam County

Sherman's left wing marched through on November 21, destroying a few miles of railroad track. A Confederate monument honoring the men and women of the Confederacy stands near the courthouse in Eatonton. On the grounds is a millstone with a WPA plaque (1936) honoring Lucius Q. C. Lamar. Born in Putnam County in

1825, he was commissioner of the Confederate government to Europe. His political career included roles as a U.S. congressman and senator from Mississippi, an associate justice of the U.S. Supreme Court, and secretary of the interior. Sherman burned Eaton-ton Factory (1833), two hundred yards from the railroad on Little River, and passed farther south to Milledgeville. Joel Chandler Harris, author of the Uncle Remus tales, witnessed Sherman's passage at Turnwold, the plantation where he started his career. William H. Seward, Lincoln's secretary of state, had operated an academy nearby as a young man.

Jones County

Weary of laying siege to Atlanta, in July 1864 Sherman sent his cavalry south to destroy Hood's vital rail links, which would have forced the city's evacuation. Gen. George Stoneman led a three-brigade force of twenty-two hundred men toward Macon, hoping to free the Union prisoners held at Andersonville. He destroyed railroad facilities and supplies in Griswoldville but was repulsed from Macon. Believing a rumor of approaching Confederate cavalry, Stoneman withdrew northward to find his path blocked by Gen. Alfred Iverson, a Clinton native, and thirteen hundred well-placed men at Sunshine Church.

Stoneman's assaults on the Confederate line were repulsed. When Iverson sent small groups of men around the Union rear, the Federal commander became convinced that he was surrounded by superior forces. Thus Stoneman ordered two brigades to withdraw while he led the third in a rear-guard action; he then ignominiously surrendered six hundred men. One of the two escaping brigades surrendered near Winder.

On November 19–22 Sherman's right wing moved through Jones County in two columns, through Blountsville and Wayside, where they burned Planters Academy.

Sunshine Church II (1880)

This replacement church stands just north of the battle site in Round Oak on GA 11. Although wounded Federals had been cared for in the original building, it was destroyed during Sherman's march.

B. F. Morris, a Federal prisoner wounded in the battle and cared for by a local family for two months, returned in 1890 to preach here. Jesse Hunt, whose wife, Mary, had nursed prisoners while he and seven brothers were serving the Confederacy, was invited to a veterans reunion dinner in Ohio. In front of Sen. John Sherman, the general's brother, Jesse carefully examined the silverware and commented, "I was just seeing if this was my wife's silver the Yankees carried off." Their daughter married Union soldier John T. Creigh, who moved south at the urging of W. F. Gladden, a Sunshine Church veteran who had purchased property nearby and helped carry Mary to her grave.

Clinton

In July 1864 two thousand Union cavalry entered the town, destroying half a million dollars' worth of property in the area before pushing on toward Macon. They returned, pursued by Confederates, and skirmished in the streets. In November five thousand Union cavalry arrived and camped in Clinton to prevent Joseph Wheeler's cavalry from harassing the Union columns. This time the fighting lasted four days. A quarter of Sherman's troops—fifteen thousand men—followed, burning a third of the town.

Judson Kilpatrick's headquarters were in the Parrish-Billue House (1810). The Iverson-Edge House (1821) was home to Alfred Iverson, who had defeated McCook at Sunshine Church, literally defending his home. His father had been a U.S. senator. The old jail (1843), burned by the Federals, was repaired, then dismantled in 1905 and the original granite blocks used to construct a retaining wall around the courthouse in Gray. Reenactments of Sunshine Church and Griswoldville and encampments are held on the first weekend in May during Old Clinton War Days, when the historical society sponsors Civil War exhibits at the McCarthy-Pope House (1808). An outstanding self-guided tour to forty points of interest, including twelve antebellum buildings, is provided by the Old Clinton Historical Society (P.O. Box 341, Gray, GA 31032). Samuel Griswold died in 1867 and is buried in the Clinton Cemetery behind the Methodist church. *Clinton is one and one-half miles southwest of Gray, just off U.S. 129, or nine miles north of Macon.*

A boulder monument at the courthouse in Gray honors Confederate veterans. The town is named for James M. Gray, who clothed

Most of Clinton was burned during two Federal raids, but the McCarthy-Pope House remains.

a local infantry company and fed the homeless and soldiers' families during the war.

Griswoldville

Now called Griswold, in the southern part of the county, this was an important Civil War manufacturing center. Samuel Griswold had established several factories along the railroad, including one that produced cotton gins that he converted in 1862 to manufacture Colt navy pistols. On November 21, 1864, Kilpatrick destroyed flour, saw, and gristmills, an iron foundry, and loaded train cars. He returned the next day but was driven off by Confederate cavalry. Reinforced by Union infantry, Kilpatrick regained the town until several units of Georgia Militia arrived. The Federal brigade withdrew a mile and entrenched on a ridge east of town. The two Georgia brigades, consisting of old men and boys and led by incompetents, launched several determined but foolhardy assaults against the Union line, losing 532 men while inflicting only 92 casualties on the Federals.

Henderson Road Baptist Church in Griswold occupies the site of the pistol factory. A gristmill pond remains. The railroad crossing was at the center of the town and its industries. The Confederates formed along the road south to GA 57 and attacked east. The Union line extended from the railroad to the south, and the battlefield was between Battle Line Branch Creek and Little Sandy Creek.

The Association for the Preservation of Civil War Sites (APCWS) has recently purchased the heart of the battlefield, eighteen and one-half acres, and granted it to the state. Plans are for a parking area and interpretive signs at the rural location, unchanged since the war. This was the only significant battle on Sherman's march.

Jarrell Plantation State Historic Site

This was a working farm from 1847 through the 1940s. During the March to the Sea the plantation was stripped thoroughly by Sherman's bummers. It has been preserved and provides a sense of the food production facilities looted and destroyed by Union troops. *Route 2, Box 220, Jarrell Plantation Road, Juliette, GA 31046 (912) 986-5172.*

Hancock County

Some of Sherman's soldiers passed through the western part of the county. A flag-draped obelisk was dedicated on April 26, 1881, and stands in front of the courthouse in Sparta. The granite was quarried locally. Beside the courthouse is the LaFayette Hotel, which housed refugees during the war.

Milledgeville

This was Georgia's capital in January 1861 when a convention to consider secession from the United States was held in the State House. Eloquent arguments for secession and for remaining in the Union were presented to Georgia's most distinguished leaders. In addition to Alexander Stephens, Robert Toombs, Benjamin Harvey Hill, Francis S. Bartow, and Thomas R. R. Cobb, the delegates included former governors, judges, and members of the U.S. Congress. When the convention voted to secede on January 19, there was a torchlight parade through the city and candles burned in most

windows to indicate support for the action. The legislative committee that wrote the Ordinance of Secession met at the Old State Bank
at East Greene and South Wilkinson.

Sherman's left wing camped outside the city on November 22.
Discovering that he was at the plantation of Howell Cobb, the president of the secession convention in Montgomery, Sherman had it
burned. The site today is a crossroads named Cobb. There was no
opposition on the following day as thirty thousand Federal soldiers
marched into the city arrayed in ranks with flags flying and bands
playing. Sherman allowed surprisingly little damage to the city;
however, the arsenal and magazine, the depot, and the Oconee
River bridge were destroyed; the library was plundered; and the
soldiers threw the desks of the legislators out of the capitol, where
they held a mock session of the legislature and "repealed" the Ordinance of Secession that had been approved in that chamber four
years earlier. The legislative antics amused Sherman. The army
rested here for several days before starting the second half of the
march to Savannah.

The Georgia College campus occupies the site of the state penitentiary. Many of the inmates had been taken into the militia before
Sherman arrived. The remaining prisoners burned the penitentiary
following their release by Union troops. The city auditorium was
used as a Confederate hospital during 1864. Nearby Oglethorpe University suspended classes when most faculty and students, including
poet Sidney Lanier, joined the Confederate army. The university
became a military hospital.

In May 1865 Varina Davis, first lady of the Confederacy,
camped nearby for a night.

Old Governors Mansion. Built in 1833, this structure was home to
ten Georgia governors, including Joseph Brown during the war.
Sherman stayed here during his brief visit, sleeping in his bedroll on
the floor (Brown had stripped the mansion of all furnishings). Federal troops arrested Brown here in May 1865. The beautiful Greek
Revival home, a National Historic Landmark, is fully restored.

Pres. Andrew Johnson appointed Unionist James Johnson provisional governor on June 29, 1865. In October a constitutional convention wrote a virtually identical copy of the Secessionist

The old governors mansion in Milledgeville was vacated as Sherman's army approached. The general slept on the floor of the mansion.

document. This recalcitrant action contributed to the fact that Atlanta was designated in 1867 as the site for another convention to compose a new constitution as required by Reconstruction legislation. The state capital was officially moved to Atlanta one year later. *120 South Clark Street, on the Georgia College Campus, P.O. Box 517, Milledgeville, GA 31061 (912) 453-4545.*

State Capitol Building. Considered to be the oldest public building in the nation, the Gothic-style capitol housed the General Assembly from 1803 to 1868. The central part dates from its completion in 1807 and the wings to 1828 and 1837. The building was reconstructed after a fire in 1941 and is now part of Georgia Military College. It houses classrooms, administrative offices, and a museum containing Civil War material. The beautiful gates at three entrances to the campus were constructed immediately after the war with bricks from the destroyed arsenal and magazine, which stood near the Presbyterian church on State Square. In front of the north gate is a Confederate monument, an obelisk with the figures of two soldiers at the base, dedicated on April 26, 1912. Sherman's Provost Guard, which kept order in the city, camped on the grounds. The other twenty-five thousand men stayed on a plantation over November

22–25, east of the Oconee River on GA 27. *Georgia Military College, 201 East Greene Street, Milledgeville, GA 31061 (912) 453-4545 (Old Governor's Mansion).*

Memory Hill Cemetery. Buried here are 479 Civil War veterans, including 24 unknowns in one section, 3 Union soldiers elsewhere, and Nathan C. Barnett, who hid the state seal when Sherman occupied the capitol. Gen. George P. Doles (1830–64) is also interred here; he was killed during the fighting around Petersburg. The county's first Confederate memorial (1868), an obelisk, was erected here.

Saint Stephen's Episcopal Church (1841). The church suffered some abuse during Sherman's occupation when it was used to quarter horses (hoof prints on the floors remain), and soldiers poured molasses into the pipe organ to "sweeten" the sound. The original roof was damaged when the magazine exploded. *210 South Wayne Street, Milledgeville, GA 31061 (912) 452-9394.*

The Tomlinson Fort-Exchange Bank House (231 West Greene Street, 1820) was headquarters of the Ladies Relief Society, which sewed shirts, socks, and underwear for Confederate soldiers. While a Confederate captain was home on leave, he had to hide in the attic when Federal troops stayed in a downstairs bedroom in the William-Orne-Crawford-Salles House (Liberty and Washington). Some historians believe many artifacts remain in the Oconee River, where Union soldiers dumped seventeen wagonloads of rifles, cannon, and shells from the arsenal. Little has been recovered.

An outstanding guide to thirty buildings in Milledgeville is available, and two-hour guided trolley tours are offered. *Baldwin County Tourism and Trade, 200 West Hancock Street, P.O. Box 219, Milledgeville, GA 31061 (912) 452-4687.*

Wilkinson County

In July 1864 Stoneman's cavalry entered Gordon to destroy the depot and 11 locomotives and 140 cars loaded with supplies for Hood's army. They torched other railroad facilities at McIntyre and Toombsboro. When Sherman's army arrived other structures were burned, and Gordon was virtually leveled. On November 21 Sherman's right wing began to converge on Gordon, Toombsboro, McIntyre, and Irwinton, where they briefly rested to prepare for the final push to Savannah.

Beside the depot in Gordon is a stone marker commemorating the foolish bravery of Rufus Kelly, a local man convalescing at home from wounds suffered in Virginia. When the Georgia Militia abandoned Gordon, Kelly fired on the advancing Union column alone and was captured. Sentenced to death, he escaped into one of the area swamps.

The courthouse in Irwinton was torched, but official records had been hidden in a nearby swamp for safekeeping.

Confederate resistance appeared as the Federals neared the Oconee River. The railroad bridge at Jackson's Ferry was blocked on the eastern side by determined Confederate infantry, so the entire column was forced to cross at Ball's Ferry. Union troops forded the Oconee there and drove off the Confederates, who were then reinforced and threw the Federals back across the river. Massive Union forces finally secured a crossing on the eastern bank.

A stone monument at a picnic area on GA 57 west of the Oconee River honors the Confederate defense of Ball's Ferry. The dirt road beside it leads to a boat landing at the ferry site where the Federal right wing crossed on two pontoon bridges. Jackson's Ferry is inaccessible in a swamp. Jefferson Davis briefly camped here the night of May 6, 1865, before leaving to search for his wife's party, rumored to be threatened by raiders.

Ramah Church. In 1861 a Confederate military unit known as the Ramah Guards was raised here and left for the battlefields of Virginia. Many of the men are buried in the adjacent cemetery. *South of Gordon on GA 57 just east of the intersection with GA 18.*

Washington County

Both wings of Sherman's army marched into Washington—the left wing from Milledgeville via Hebron and the right from Ball's Ferry by way of Irwin's Crossroads. The left wing's advance was slowed by skirmishes with Confederate cavalry who also burned numerous bridges over Buffalo Creek. Railroad facilities in Tennille were destroyed.

Sandersville

Because Confederate solders fought in the streets of Sandersville and the townspeople seized and executed several captive Federals, Sherman ordered the commercial and government buildings burned.

The Museum of Washington County. The museum is behind the courthouse in the old 1891 jail. Among the Civil War artifacts is a couch from the William Brown House on which Sherman spent the night of November 26. The house survives on North Harris Street. *313 South Harris Street, P.O. Box 692 (31-81), Sandersville, GA 31082 (912) 552-6965.*

A Confederate memorial erected in 1879 is at the city cemetery. Union soldiers are believed to be buried in an unmarked raised brick crypt.

With John H. Reagan (acting treasury secretary) and Capt. M. H. Clark (acting treasurer), Jefferson Davis conducted the last official business of the Confederacy in Sandersville at noon on May 6, 1865. His passage is marked by a small monument in front of the courthouse, which was erected in 1868 on the original foundation of the courthouse burned during the March to the Sea. A monument to Gov. Jared Irwin bears bullet scars from skirmishing in the streets. Only two structures survived on the square; one of them is the public library (131 West Haynes Street, 1856).

Davis had spent the previous night in the woods near Griffin's Pond, north of Sandersville on GA 15 and one and one-half miles south of Warthen, where the party had stopped to buy food. A hand-hewn log jail (1794) held Aaron Burr in 1804.

Oconee was known as Station #14, a railroad stop. It was visited by William J. Hardee, who then authorized abandonment of the Oconee River line. It survives as a near ghost town on the railroad near the river. The Seventeenth Corps moved through Tennille (Station #13) and Riddleville. A small shaft with two flanking cannon was dedicated in 1907 on Main Street beside the Tennille police station. It once had a frosted illuminated globe, the only known electrified

Confederate monument. Here Sherman joined the right wing. Nearby was Tarvers Mill, whose rural beauty impressed the Federals.

Johnson County

At the intersection of GA 57 and GA 68 in Washington County, Oliver O. Howard's Fifteenth Corps turned south through Wrightsville, Kite, Summerville, and Cannochee, at one point losing their way. On November 28 part of Sherman's right wing raided farther south, stripping the land of livestock. SR 622, the Old Savannah Road, was taken by Sherman and the Seventeenth Corps to the Ogeechee.

Dublin

On May 7, 1865, Jefferson Davis crossed the Oconee River via ferry, closely pursued by Union cavalry. The Georgia Warehouse and Compress Company, on the north side of Madison, marks the site of his camp. Davis found his wife, Varina, at Blackshear Plantation, ten miles north of Dublin.

A Confederate monument is on U.S. 80 in front of the old Carnegie Library. Note that the soldier is in the process of opening a powder flask, which was largely a pre–Civil War action. The Laurens County Historical Society maintains a museum in the former library, where some Confederate material is displayed. *Dublin-Laurens Museum, Bellevue and Academy Avenues, P.O. Box 140, Dublin, GA 31021 (912) 272-9242.*

Twiggs County

Warned of Sherman's approach by Wheeler, area residents hid their livestock and lost little to Federal cavalry.

Jeffersonville. A Confederate monument dedicated in 1911 is on U.S. 80 opposite the railroad tracks. Although a foundation had been prepared for the memorial at the courthouse, a lawsuit over who had or had not served the Confederacy arose and the monument was relegated to this less-than-official perch.

Richland Baptist Church (1811). In June 1861 church women sewed a flag and made first aid kits for the Twiggs Guard. *Three miles southeast of Marion.*

Jefferson County

The left wing crossed the Ogeechee at Fenn's Bridge and proceeded through Davisboro, which was burned, to Louisville on November 27. Louisville was almost totally destroyed by looters, and only a slave market (late 1700s) remains of the Civil War community that was once Georgia's capital. The Federals rounded up all the useful mounts in the area and then shot the rest.

In the city cemetery (Seventh Street and Academy Drive) is the grave of Confederate Gen. Reuben W. Carswell (1838–89). He fought in the Seven Days, Second Manassas, Antietam, Fredericksburg, Chancellorsville, Gettysburg, Wilderness, and Cold Harbor campaigns. Carswell was called home with the Georgia Militia to resist Sherman's march to Savannah. He was captured and paroled in Augusta in May 1865.

To the south is Bartow (Spier's Turnout), renamed for Confederate Gen. Francis S. Bartow. Two sons of the founder, William Spier, both killed in the war, rest in the city cemetery.

Burke County

The right wing crossed the Ogeechee at Midville on November 30. Hoping to convince the Confederates that he was advancing on Augusta, Sherman sent Kilpatrick's cavalry north to burn bridges over Brier Creek on the Augusta Road. When Kilpatrick attempted to complete this mission on November 27, Wheeler assaulted him repeatedly and drove the Federal cavalry into Jenkins County. On December 2 Kilpatrick returned, accompanied by an infantry division, which drove Wheeler out of Waynesboro and burned the bridges.

Burke County Museum. This museum features a collection of Civil War artifacts, some of them retrieved locally. The courthouse (1857), partially burned by Kilpatrick, was rebuilt. Two Civil War cannon guard the entrance. *536 Liberty Street, one block south of U.S. 25, Waynesboro, GA 30830 (706) 554-4889.*

In the old city cemetery (Jones and Sixth) is a Confederate monument, an obelisk dedicated April 26, 1877. It is surrounded by the graves of forty-nine unidentified Confederates and twelve Union troopers who died fighting in Waynesboro.

Shell Bluff, a unique geological feature consisting of millions of giant fossilized oyster shells deposited in a layer 150 feet long and 40 feet wide sixty million years ago, overlooks the Savannah River. During the Civil War Confederates established a battery here and placed torpedoes and pilings in the river to obstruct the waterway and protect Augusta, eighty miles upriver. When Sherman threatened Augusta, eighteen men were dispatched to man the single 8-inch Columbiad, but they found it and the stored munitions in poor condition. This was the home of James Madison Gray, an important Confederate financier. *Off GA 17 thirteen miles northeast of Waynesboro.*

North of Waynesboro is Brier Creek, where the bridges were burned and skirmishes fought. To the south, three miles west of U.S. 25 between Waynesboro and Millen, is war-scarred Bellevue Plantation (1768), one of Georgia's oldest. While the plantation was crowded with refugees from the fighting in Waynesboro, cavalry clashed on the grounds. Two towns visited by Union troops, Munnerlyn and Thomas Station, are found between Waynesboro and Millen.

Jenkins County

The right wing passed through in the first days of December, stripping the country of food and destroying the depot, hotel, and warehouses in Millen. At the courthouse is a Confederate monument, unveiled in June 1909, and a boulder marking the site of a wayside home, where traveling soldiers were assisted during the war. South of Millen on U.S. 25 is a monument erected to the memory of several soldiers who died at the wayside. The depot (Cotton Street, 1917) is a recreation on the site of the original, which was torched in 1864.

Magnolia Springs Prison. To help relieve the overcrowding and deadly conditions at Andersonville, Confederate officials built Camp

Lawton at Magnolia Springs, where seven million gallons of pure water flows daily. It was the South's largest POW camp, intended to hold 40,000 men within its forty-three enclosed acres. The stockade was ringed by forty sentry boxes and earthworks that contained eleven cannon. The prison housed only 10,279 prisoners, and the 500 to 700 who died were later reinterred at Andersonville. When Sherman marched east, the prisoners were evacuated to camps in southern Georgia and South Carolina. Union troops angrily torched the empty prison, which had been occupied for only 113 days.

Magnolia Springs is today a state park. The prison site remains, highlighted by the earthworks. Two timbers from the stockade are displayed. Adjacent is the Ginn National Fish Hatchery and Aquarium, which makes use of the abundant spring water that supplied the prison. *Five miles north of Millen on U.S. 25. Magnolia Springs State Park, Route 5, Box 458, Millen, GA 30442 (912) 982-1660.*

Buckhead Church. When Wheeler drove Kilpatrick from the Brier Creek bridges on November 27, the Federals crossed Buckhead Creek to make a stand. Wheeler's dismounted cavalry attacked the

Cavalry battles raged around this rural Buckhead church, and its pews were removed to bridge a nearby creek.

Federal line at several points, forcing Kilpatrick to withdraw to Millen. Beautiful historic Buckhead Church stands near the creek. The church pews that Wheeler used to replace the burned span still retain hoof prints. *One mile north of CR 79 on CR 81, northwest of Millen.*

Nearby, surrounded by lanes lined with ancient oaks, is one of Georgia's premier plantations, Birdsville (1781; Greek Revival front 1847). It originally claimed sixty-six thousand acres and had many outbuildings. Federals, including Sherman, remained here for several days. While searching for treasure in the family cemetery, they dug up the twin sons recently born to Mrs. William B. Jones. Legend says that the house was set afire, but Mrs. Jones refused to leave her sickbed, forcing Union soldiers to extinguish the fire.

Screven County

Here Sherman's forces began to converge on Savannah. The right wing marched along both sides of the Ogeechee River and destroyed the railroad while the left wing moved down from the north through Sylvania. Confederate forces dispatched from Savannah established a defensive line at Oliver (Ogeechee Church), but the approach of both Federal columns compelled the small force to withdraw.

At Memorial Cemetery in Sylvania is a Confederate monument, dedicated April 26, 1899, and two cannon.

Sherman and the Seventeenth Corps paralleled GA 17 and the Ogeechee through Paramore, Scarboro, Rocky Ford, Ogeechee, Cooperville, Cameron, and Oliver. Little remains today of these communities. The Fifteenth Corps marched through Mill Ray in Bulloch County.

On the left wing, the Fourteenth Corps struggled along the Old Savannah Road, paralleling the Savannah River and contending with constant skirmishes and wretched road conditions. The Twentieth Corps marched comfortably on the Middle Ground Road.

Bulloch County

One of Sherman's columns passed through on December 4–5. There was a brief skirmish at the Statesboro city limits on U.S. 80 West when Confederates assaulted foraging Federal cavalry, but infantry came up to drive the Southerners off.

At the courthouse (the 1807 wooden original was burned by Sherman) in Statesboro is a Confederate monument erected in 1909. The Jackal Hotel at 67 East Main Street hosted a reunion of one hundred Confederate veterans and two thousand locals on July 19, 1911.

Jenks Bridge, on U.S. 80 at the Ogeechee River, is where the Fifteenth Corps forced a crossing. From this point to Savannah, the Confederates barricaded the roads with felled trees, harassed the column with cannon fire from emplacements and rail cars, and mined the road.

Effingham County

On December 8–10 most of Sherman's force moved through the county, the right wing through Eden, the left wing through Springfield. The Fourteenth Corps camped at historic Ebenezer Church (1768) on the Savannah River. On nearby Ebenezer Creek, swollen from the winter rains, Union Gen. Jefferson C. Davis prevented hundreds of runaway slaves from crossing. The terrified refugees panicked and ran into the water; dozens died and the remainder were captured by Confederate cavalry. Between Ebenezer and Clyo, to the north, is Sister's Ferry, where half of Sherman's force crossed the Savannah to invade South Carolina in January 1865.

An obelisk at the courthouse in Springfield, unveiled April 26, 1923, honors local Confederate veterans. Long stretches of road in the county are bordered by swamp, and Sherman's men grew hungry and miserable marching through this poor region.

Guyton

Several hospitals operated in this railroad town during the war, including one at the United Methodist Church (Fourth Avenue,

1846). The Confederacy established a basic training camp here and a depot at the vital rail junction. In the city cemetery behind the high school on Cemetery Road is a Confederate section for men who died of wounds or disease. To the south, at Zion Church, Sherman spent a night.

Bryan County

On December 9 retreating Confederates burned King's Bridge on the Ogeechee River between Richmond Hill and Savannah. It was rebuilt and on December 12 Union Gen. William B. Hazen camped here on his way to attack Fort McAllister. With the river open, Sherman built a long wharf and storehouses to receive large quantities of supplies from Federal ships during the siege of Savannah. Before seizing the position, Capt. William Duncan and two men in a canoe silently paddled past Confederate sentries with messages from Sherman to the navy. It was the first word the North had received from Sherman in six weeks. King's Bridge is now a recreational area on the northern side of the U.S. 17 bridge.

Over December 6–8 Federal skirmishers fought their way across the Ogeechee and Canoochee Rivers to Richmond Hill, known then as Cross Roads and Way's Station, where the Gulf Railroad was broken. Fort McAllister was isolated, and Union troops turned east to attack it.

Fort McAllister

This fort was the southernmost defense of Savannah, built to protect a back route through the Ogeechee River. It consisted of gun emplacements separated by strong earthen walls. Inside were large bombproofs—timber-supported shelters covered with dirt that housed magazines and supply rooms. The fort mounted one siege gun, twelve field pieces, and a mortar. The river was obstructed with pilings and torpedoes.

After the fall of Fort Pulaski, McAllister became a symbol of valor in Georgia, withstanding seven attacks in 1863 by Union monitors and gunboats. The ironclads repeatedly pressed close to shore and hurled hundreds of shots into the fort, creating enormous craters that were easily filled with sand. Despite the intensive bombardments, McAllister's gunners stood by their cannon and bounced shots off the ships.

After a final fruitless attack by three ironclads, three gunboats, and mortarboats, the Federal navy decided that McAllister was impregnable and left it alone. They did succeed in destroying the *Nashville,* a blockade-runner converted to a commerce raider that had grounded near the fort.

Sherman had to capture Fort McAllister so the blockading fleet could provide supplies for his army. Although the small garrison of 230 men fought heroically during the attack on December 13, waves of Federal infantry poured over the works and subdued the defenders. With McAllister in enemy hands, Savannah had to be evacuated.

Abandoned after the war, Fort McAllister deteriorated. In the 1930s Henry Ford built a home nearby and had the fort restored. Georgia acquired the site in 1958 to establish a state park. The earthworks have been impressively preserved, bombproofs have been reconstructed to wartime condition and outfitted as powder magazines and barracks, and guns have been mounted. Detached from the fort is a mortar battery, connected by a long earthen wall to facilitate safe movement during attack. A walking tour conducts visitors across the moat to the gun positions and bombproofs. Exhibits in the museum illustrate the history of the fort, including an impressive diorama depicting its fall and artifacts salvaged from the *Nashville.*

A plaque pays homage to Tom Cat, the fort mascot who was the only casualty of the March 3, 1863, ironclad attack. His loss was noted in the Savannah newspapers and official reports. *Fort McAllister State Historic Park is east of I-95 on GA Spur 144; 394-A Fort McAllister Road, P.O. Box 198, Richmond Hill, GA 31324 (912) 727-2339.*

Lebanon Plantation (1804), between Savannah and Fort McAllister, was owned by Maj. George W. Anderson, commander of the fort. He and Hazen, who led the troops who stormed the fort, were old West Point friends. At a dinner hosted by Anderson for his enemy, a toast was offered to the courageous Union attackers and Confederate defenders. Strathy Hall, home of Confederate Lt. Col. Joseph L.

Federal troops swarmed over this corner of Fort McAllister (above) to open a supply route with the navy. Earth-covered bombproofs (below) protected the fort's stores and hospital during bombardments from Union ironclads.

McAllister (the fort was on his land and named for his father), was used as Judson Kilpatrick's headquarters on December 12. The home is in Strathy Hall Estates off GA 144 between Richmond Hill and GA Spur 144.

Kilkenny Bluff. Now the site of a marina, Kilpatrick rode here to contact the Union fleet in Saint Catherine's Sound. *At the end of Kilkenny Bluff Road off GA 144.*

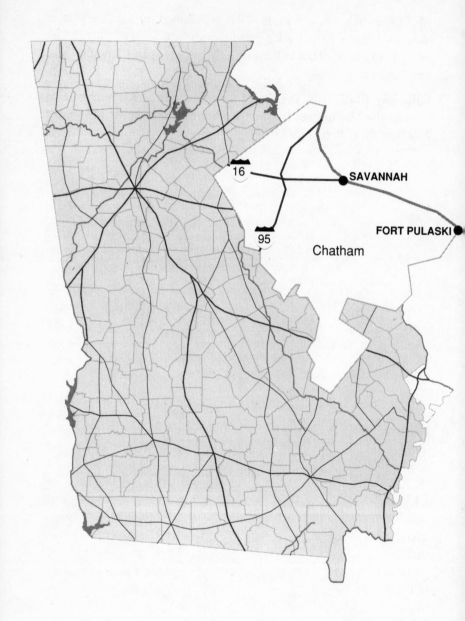

7

Savannah

WHEN GEORGIA SECEDED from the Union, Savannah became an important port for the Confederacy. An effective Federal blockade, however, soon closed the city to all but a few daring blockade-runners. With the capture of Fort Pulaski in 1862, the noose was drawn even more tightly, and fears were ignited that an assault on the city was imminent from the Federals occupying nearby Hilton Head, South Carolina. The attack never materialized, partly because the Confederates erected extensive fortifications to cover every water approach to the city.

When Sherman began his March to the Sea in November 1864, Confederate Gen. William J. Hardee was charged with the defense of Savannah. He established a strong line of defensive works facing west. When Sherman arrived on December 11 with his sixty-thousand-man army, Federal forces encircled the city to cut off any avenue of escape and then pressed ever closer toward the Confederate positions.

After the fall of Fort McAllister, Sherman opened a supply base at Kings Bridge on the Ogeechee River and ordered up large siege guns. He did not intend to assault the formidable Confederate defenses but decided to batter down the majestic city and starve the garrison into surrender—just as he had done outside Atlanta.

Hardee deceived Sherman through an ingenious plan to evacuate his men, laying a makeshift pontoon bridge from Savannah to two islands and finally to the South Carolina shore. On the night of December 20 his ten thousand men spiked their guns and withdrew from the city. Sherman was dumbfounded by their escape but pleased to capture the city intact.

It was in Savannah that Charles C. Cevor had constructed a famous observation balloon used by the Confederates in Virginia during the Peninsula and Seven Days campaigns.

On February 1, 1879, Sherman arrived in Savannah as part of an overall inspection of the country's military facilities. One result of that tour was the decision to close Oglethorpe Barracks and reassign the troops to Atlanta.

Downtown Savannah

Savannah History Museum. Housed in the old Central of Georgia Railroad passenger terminal (1860) with the Savannah visitors center, the museum offers an exciting display of history in a number of Civil War exhibits, including figures of soldiers from Savannah's militia units—the Irish Jasper Greens and the Republican Blues— material relating to Francis S. Bartow (a native son who died at First Manassas), the bombardment of Fort Pulaski, the capture of the city, and other artifacts. The walls are full of period photographs and artwork portraying Civil War Savannah. Many of the city's young men marched off to war serenaded by bands and accompanied by great festivities. Soon anxious crowds gathered at the railroad station to read the lengthening lists of casualties and retrieve the bodies returned from distant battlefields. The facility is operated by the Coastal Heritage Society. *303 Martin Luther King Jr. Boulevard, Savannah, GA 31401 (912) 238-1779.*

The Savannah Central Railroad Complex (1843) is a half-block south on West Harris Street. This is the country's largest collection of original antebellum railroad buildings—five acres and thirteen structures—including a massive roundhouse and turntable, a 125-foot-high smokestack, and railroad shops for repair and maintenance, all overseen by the Coastal Heritage Society. Some of America's oldest locomotives, rolling stock, and other artifacts are on display. Visitors will recognize several settings from the Civil War movie *Glory. The Central of Georgia Railroad Roundhouse Complex, 301 West Harris Street, Savannah, GA 31401 (912) 651-6823.*

Green-Medrim House (1853). This house, which served as Sherman's headquarters, is now the parish house of Saint John's Church and is open to the public. The owner offered Sherman the use of the house to spare a Southern woman from having her home commandeered, although some say that the merchant was attempting to save his cotton. General Hardee's brother visited Sherman here, as did Gustavus W. Smith's wife and treasury agent A. G. Browne. Browne suggested that Sherman offer the city to Lincoln as the famous Christmas gift of 1864. Sherman and his staff enjoyed a lavish Christmas dinner here. After the war Green hosted Robert E. Lee's son, Gen. Fitzhugh Lee. *West side of Madison Square at Bull Street; Saint John's Church, 1 West Macon Street, Savannah, GA 31401 (912) 232-1251; (912) 233-3845.*

When Robert E. Lee stopped in Savannah on April 18, 1870, while on his last visit to his father's grave on Cumberland Island, he was met at the train station by Alexander R. Lawton and taken to his home at Lincoln and York (228 East York Street). West Broad Street was crowded with people desiring to glimpse their former leader and pay their respects. After Lee's death on October 17, a large meeting was held in Johnson Square to plan a memorial service. On April 19, 1871, a parade was led by Joseph E. Johnston and nine other Confederate generals and followed by virtually the entire population, which proceeded to Forsyth Park for the ceremony. Lee had visited the Francis Sorrel House (northwest corner of Bull and Harris, 1841) while working on Fort Pulaski as a young man.

Comer House. Jefferson Davis and his daughter Winnie stayed in this Victorian home (1880, now a bed and breakfast) during a visit to Savannah in 1886 for the centennial celebration of the Chatham Artillery, one of America's oldest artillery units. A committee of Savannahians, including G. Moxley Sorrel, accompanied Davis from Atlanta on May 3, and his stay was remembered as a "continuous ovation." The former president received many tributes and outpourings of emotion from crowds at the festivities. Things had changed considerably since the late 1860s when Varina Davis and her children, who lived here after the war, had been subjected to constant ridicule while the former Southern president was imprisoned. *2 East Taylor Street, on the northeastern corner of Bull and Taylor Streets, Savannah, GA 31401 (912) 234-2923.*

Second African Baptist Church. On January 16, 1865, Sherman issued Order #150 from here, appropriating the coastal islands of Georgia and South Carolina for freed slaves, who were promised "forty acres and a mule." Pres. Andrew Johnson nullified the proclamation nine months later. *123 Houston Street.*

Juliette Gordon Low Birthplace (1820). The founder of the Girl Scouts of America had relatives from her mother's side fighting for the Union. The house of the prominent Lows was visited by Sherman and Oliver O. Howard, who, with the young girl on his knee, explained how he had lost his arm in battle. "Oh, I bet that was my papa," Juliette innocently said. "He has shot lots of Yankees." *142 Bull Street at Oglethorpe Avenue, Savannah, GA 31401 (912) 233-4501.*

The Washington Guns are on Broad Street. They were captured from the British at Yorktown and presented in 1791 by George Washington to the Chatham Artillery during his celebrated visit to the South. At the outbreak of the Civil War the bronze 9-pounders were buried for safekeeping beneath the armory and not retrieved until 1872, when Federal occupation troops withdrew.

Savannah Historical Society. In the society's collection is a Joe Brown pike and a clock captured from a Union ship by a Confederate raider. *501 Gaston Street, Savannah, GA 31401 (912) 944-2128.*

Ships of the Sea Museum. Among the fascinating naval artifacts here are models of the renowned raider CSS *Alabama* and the ironclad CSS *Atlanta;* the latter features cutaway sections to reveal the interior, where a crew serves a gun and other sailors tend the boilers. *503 East River Street and 504 East Bay Street, Savannah, GA 31401 (912) 232-1511.*

At Bull and East Bay Streets is the Greek Revival U.S. Customs House (1850) which Sherman climbed for a view of his prize. Throughout Reconstruction, Federal headquarters were next door at 7 Bay Street. Across the street, now occupied by the city hall, is the site of the city exchange, where Federals arrived to occupy the city at 6 A.M. on December 21, 1864.

The end of West Broad Street where it dead-ends at River Street is the site of the pontoon bridge over which Hardee's troops escaped.

At the top of the bluff on Bay Street is the spot where Union artillery unlimbered to fire ineffectually on the ironclad *Savannah* that morning. The Savannah Arsenal, which was destroyed by a deadly fire in January 1865, was at Broad and Broughton Streets.

The former Warren A. Candler Hospital, part of it dating to 1819, at Drayton and East Huntingdon Streets, cared for wounded Confederates. In 1864 a stockade was built around the rear to contain Union prisoners. After the war, Joseph E. Johnston made Savannah his home (105 East Oglethorpe Avenue, 1821) for several years while he worked as an insurance agent. The home of Gen. G. Moxley Sorrel, aide to James Longstreet, is at Harris and Bull, on Madison Square. Sorrel's childhood home, the Sorrel-Weed House, is at Bull and Macon. The Pink House (23 Abercorn Street, 1789) was the headquarters of Federal occupation forces in 1865. River Street was filmed for the Boston parade scene in *Glory,* and the streets around Monterey Square, where only one house is not nineteenth century, were covered with sand for *Glory* and *His Name Was Mudd.* The city has twenty wonderful squares filled with impressive monuments. They were used as campsites by many of Sherman's men.

Maj. John B. Gallie, killed by the monitor *Montauk* at Fort McAllister on February 1, 1863, and buried at Laurel Grove Cemetery, lived at the southeast corner of Charlton and Abercorn. Francis S. Bartow, hero of Manassas and commander of the Oglethorpe Light Infantry, lived at the northeast corner of Barnard and Harris (126 West Harris Street, 1842).

Occupation commander Oliver O. Howard and his successor, Gen. William F. Barry, stayed in the home at the northeast corner of Bull and Gaston (1857). The British owners, who sold the house to Confederate Gen. Henry R. Jackson in 1885, claimed that ten thousand dollars' worth of property had been damaged or stolen during the occupation. The Massie School (1853) at the southeast corner of Gordon and Abercorn was a Union hospital and then a school for the education of freedmen. The Sisters of Mercy who operated the Convent and Academy of Saint Vincent DePaul (207 East Liberty Street) nursed sick and wounded Confederates. The children of Jefferson Davis attended the school after the war.

When word was received of South Carolina's secession in December 1860, a wild public celebration was held in Johnson

Square (1733), where the Palmetto flag was waved from the top of the impressive Greene Monument. That night Maj. C. C. Jones addressed a delirious crowd in Pulaski Square from the balcony of Pulaski House, where Sherman spent his first night in the city almost exactly four years later. It is now the site of a cafeteria.

Eliza Thompson Inn. Fearing Union troops would torch her house (1847, now a bed and breakfast), Eliza Thompson baked cakes to sell to the Federals in Madison Square, earning money and pacifying Yankee hearts. *5 West Jones Street, Savannah, GA 31401 (912) 236-3630.*

Savannah's Confederate monument is one of the most ornate in the country.

Mercer-Wilder House. Begun in 1860 by Gen. Hugh Mercer, the house was unfinished when Sherman arrived. Union soldiers stripped it of timber to build shanties in the squares. It was featured in *Glory* as the Boston home of Robert Gould Shaw. *427 Bull Street at Monterey Square.*

Savannah's imposing Confederate monument stands in twenty-acre Forsyth Park on Bull Street between Gaston Street and Park Avenue. It was commissioned by the Ladies Memorial Association. Designed by Robert Reid of Montreal and made of Canadian sandstone, it was shipped by sea so it would not touch Yankee soil. Around it are bronze busts of two Savannah Confederate heroes, Francis S. Bartow and LaFayette McLaws. The original monument, dedicated on May 24, 1875, was deemed excessively ornate. It was simplified by replacing the life-sized marble figures of Judgment and Justice with a statue of a soldier. Ironically, the bronze soldier was designed by a

Northerner, David Richards, and cast in New York. At a cost of thirty-five thousand dollars, this was Georgia's most expensive war memorial. Forsyth Park was a parade ground and campground during the war.

Cemeteries

Laurel Grove Cemetery. In the Gettysburg plot the Silence Monument watches over the graves of 700 Confederate soldiers. During 1871–73 Dr. Rufus Weaver of Philadelphia opened Confederate graves at Gettysburg and sent the remains of 101 Georgians to Savannah; other remains were dispatched to Richmond, Wilmington, and Charleston. The other soldiers buried here died on garrison duty, in Savannah's trenches, or defending Fort McAllister. Union soldiers killed around Savannah are interred at the nearby Beaufort National Cemetery in South Carolina. Recently the plot's crumbling sandstone headstones have been replaced with marble headstones. The Confederate Veterans Association Monument, a cannon set on a stone base, and the McLaws Camp 596 Monument, an obelisk, were also erected in the cemetery. The brochure *A Tour of Savannah's Necropoli* is very useful.

Most prominent among the one Union and seven Confederate generals buried here is Francis S. Bartow (1816–61) who attended the Georgia secession convention and helped form the Confederacy in Montgomery, Alabama. As chairman of the committee on military affairs, he decided that Southern soldiers would wear gray uniforms. He led the Oglethorpe Light Infantry to Virginia on May 21, 1861, in direct violation of orders from Gov. Joseph Brown, who believed that state troops should not leave the state. At First Manassas on July 20, Bartow led the Seventh, Eighth, and Twenty-first Georgia Infantry Regiments. Outnumbered three to one, he and Barnard Bee of South Carolina suffered horrendous casualties while buying time for reinforcements to arrive. Moments after giving Thomas J. Jackson his immortal nickname, Bee was mortally wounded and Bartow was killed. In Richmond, Varina Davis delivered the news to Bartow's wife. The two fallen generals lay in state in Richmond for two days.

The Savannah city council planned Bartow's funeral. A large crowd met his body at the train station and followed it to the Cotton

Exchange, where it lay in state for three days before the funeral at Christ Church and its burial at Laurel Grove. Lesser-ranking Georgians killed at First Manassas were returned to Savannah during the winter of 1862.

Other generals buried here include G. Moxley Sorrel, Edward Willis, Henry C. Wayne, Jeremy R. Gilmer, Peter A. S. McGlashan, and George P. Harrison. Sorrel (1838–1901) was the brother-in-law of Confederate Gen. William W. Mackell and gained fame as Longstreet's adjutant general. Willis (1840–64) was the Confederacy's youngest brigadier. Born in Washington, Georgia, he resigned from West Point in January 1861 and was mortally wounded in the Wilderness on May 29, 1864, at the age of twenty-three. He had been engaged to marry Sorrel's sister and was buried in the Sorrel family vault. Wayne (1815–83), West Point class of 1838, wrote a manual on sword combat, experimented with the use of camels in the West, and was adjutant and inspector general with the Georgia Militia during Sherman's March to the Sea. Gilmer (1818–83), West Point class of 1839, served at Shiloh, Atlanta, and Charleston, and commanded the Confederacy's engineer corps. McGlashan (1831–1908), a Scottish adventurer, sought gold in California, attempted to overthrow the Nicaraguan government with William Walker, and served with Longstreet from Second Manassas to Sayler's Creek, where he surrendered on April 6, 1865. He claimed to have been the last brigadier appointed by Jefferson Davis, but his commission is disputed. Harrison (1814–88), a brigadier of Georgia Militia, was captured in 1864 at his home near Monteith.

Also buried here is Phoebe Pember, commemorated recently on a U.S. postage stamp. She arranged a government position through the wife of William Randolph, Confederate secretary of war, and reported in November 1861 to Chimborazo Hospital in Richmond, the world's largest, which treated seventy-six thousand soldiers. She was the last Confederate official in Richmond in April 1865, protecting her patients with a pistol until Union officers arrived. Her 1879 book, *A Southern Woman's Story: Life in Confederate Richmond,* is filled with humor and insights into political and social intrigues. She was buried here in 1913.

Another occupant is James L. Pierpoint, a Bostonian who came to Savannah in 1850 and served in the First Georgia Cavalry. In addition to "Jingle Bells," he wrote such Southern favorites as "We Conquer or Die" and "Strike for the South."

Also resting in Laurel Grove are the Confederate commanders of Forts Pulaski, Jackson, and McAllister; Charles Lamar, believed to be the last Southerner killed in combat (in Columbus a week after Lee's surrender); Anna Raines, the founder of the United Daughters of the Confederacy; and James M. Wayne, a Supreme Court justice when the Dred Scott decision was handed down, which brought the country closer to Civil War. *Laurel Grove Cemetery is on West Anderson off Martin Luther King Drive.*

Bonaventure Cemetery claims a renowned naval commander— Josiah Tattnall—and six Confederate generals—Alexander R. Lawton, LaFayette McLaws, Henry R. Jackson, Hugh W. Mercer, Claudius G. Wilson, and Robert H. Anderson. Tattnall (1795–1871), from an old Savannah family, served in the U.S. Navy from 1812 to 1861. He led the Mosquito Fleet (four armed tugboats) in a valiant effort to defend Port Royal, ordered the destruction of the ironclad *Virginia,* and commanded Savannah's naval defense against Sherman. This cemetery is part of his family's plantation. Lawton (1818–96), West Point class of 1839, married the sister of Gen. Edward Porter Alexander. He fought with Stonewall Jackson in Antietam's savage cornfield, where his brigade suffered 50 percent casualties. Lawton himself was so severely wounded that he was reassigned as quartermaster general of the army. He accompanied Jefferson Davis in the flight from Richmond and was with him when the government was dissolved at Washington, Georgia. His family has an impressive monument along the Wilmington River. McLaws (1821–97), West Point class of 1842, served with Longstreet in Virginia, at Chickamauga, and at Knoxville, where they argued. McLaws then opposed Sherman along the march to Savannah. Jackson (1820–98) served in Virginia and Tennessee before being captured at Nashville on December 15, 1864. He was president of the Georgia Historical Society here for twenty-four years. The Cobb brothers of Athens were his cousins. Mercer (1808–77), West Point class of 1828, commanded Savannah until 1864, then participated in the Atlanta campaign and served with Hardee at Savannah and in the Carolinas. Wilson (1831–63) fought at Chickamauga and died on December 26, 1863, of a fever at Ringgold. Anderson (1835–88), West Point class of 1857, was the commander of Fort McAllister. *Bonaventure Cemetery is on Bonaventure Road off Victory Drive-U.S. 80.*

The Savannah Catholic Cemetery has a small lot designated as the Daughters of the Confederacy Plot and containing the graves of eight Confederate soldiers and a small granite monument erected in their honor. Nearby is the Irish Jasper Greens Monument, a statue dedicated on April 26, 1910.

Isle of Hope Methodist Church. A four-gun battery mounting two 8-inch Columbiads and two 32-pounders was emplaced on the grounds during the war, and the structure was used as a hospital and barracks for Confederates stationed in the area. In the cemetery are thirty-three soldiers who died here, most of them volunteers from Effingham County. The original structure burned in 1984 but was faithfully reproduced. Soldiers' names and initials are carved on the original pews on which they once slept. *Parkersburg Road, Isle of Hope.*

Old Black Cemetery. Occupied by the Federals during the war, the cemetery has graves for both Confederate and Union soldiers. *At First African Baptist Church of Savannah, Franklin Square, 23 Montgomery Street, Savannah, GA 31401 (912) 233-6597.*

Another Savannah resident was James D. Bulloch (1823–1901), who joined the U.S. Navy in 1839. After resigning and accepting a Confederate commission, he traveled to Europe and purchased ships from England and France, primarily the CSS *Alabama* and the *Fingal,* which he brought personally to Savannah and converted to the ironclad *Atlanta.* Pres. Andrew Johnson sought Bulloch's arrest, but the ship purchaser became an English citizen and is buried in Liverpool.

Sherman stabled horses in historic Colonial Park Cemetery at East Oglethorpe and Abercorn Streets. Union soldiers camped here, in some instances sleeping in brick vaults emptied of their original occupants.

Forts

As an important port city, Savannah had been fortified since colonial days. Fort Jackson is downstream of the city on the Savannah River, and Fort Pulaski was constructed to command the river near the Atlantic Ocean. After Pulaski had been demolished by rifled cannon in April 1862, more than a dozen extensive earthen forts and batteries were built to defend a number of sea approaches to the city.

Many significant Civil War earthworks have completely vanished, including Fort Lee, a large fortification downstream of Fort Jackson, and Fort Thunderbolt, which is occupied by the marina below the Wilmington River bridge at Thunderbolt. Some of Sherman's troops boarded ships there for Beaufort, where they began the campaign through the Carolinas.

Local lore alleges that Savannah was the first American city where golf was played (1796). The grounds of the Savannah Golf Club incorporate Confederate earthworks from Fort Boggs as bunkers. *Just west of Fort Jackson off U.S. 80.*

Fort Jackson

This brick fort was built in the early 1800s on the main ship channel of the Savannah River just three miles below the city. It is surrounded by a nine-foot-deep tidal moat that can be crossed by a single drawbridge. The entrance was protected by two small cannon that could sweep the entrance with a crossfire of grapeshot if an enemy attempted to storm the fort.

The gun platform on top of the twenty-foot-high walls held eleven cannon that were served by men of the Twenty-second Battalion of Heavy Artillery. The fort, headquarters for the defense of Savannah, was visited by Robert E. Lee, Jefferson Davis, and P. G. T. Beauregard.

When the destruction of the much stronger Fort Pulaski demonstrated the limitation of brick forts, six earthen batteries containing thirty-six cannon were constructed on the banks of the river near Fort Jackson. When Fort McAllister fell, the garrison of Fort Jackson and the crews of the land batteries spiked their guns and withdrew to South Carolina.

Fort Jackson was abandoned following the Spanish-American War. During the 1950s it was almost broken up for brick salvage, but the Coastal Heritage Foundation purchased and preserved the fort.

In the large courtyard is the brick foundation of an officers' barracks and a recreated mess. Several small period craft are displayed in a boathouse, and a 32-pounder cannon has been mounted atop the wall. An earthen water battery was erected near the river.

Within the thick brick walls are galleries that served as powder magazines, storerooms, cells, and offices. They now house a number of exhibits concerning Savannah's Civil War history, particularly that of the Savannah ironclads. The city was protected by four ironclads similar to the *Virginia*—the *Georgia, Atlanta, Savannah,* and *Milledgeville*—which were meant to break the Union blockade of Savannah and open the shipping lanes to Europe. Unfortunately, the ponderous monoliths had severe deficiencies. Because the *Georgia* lacked engines strong enough to move its bulk, she was anchored opposite Fort Jackson and served as a floating (barely) gun platform. The *Atlanta* was captured when it attacked two Union monitors. At Sherman's approach the *Savannah* was blown up and the nearly completed *Milledgeville* burned, but the *Georgia* was merely scuttled. It remains the only relatively intact Confederate ironclad in existence. Divers have brought up artifacts from the hulk, including eight cannon, and some of the material is displayed here. Armor for the ironclads and artillery ammunition were made at the Indian Street Foundry at Yamacraw.

Fort Jackson regularly hosts special public programs concerning coastal history, including encampments of the Twenty-second Battalion of Georgia Heavy Artillery (CSA, Recreated). The fort has also started a School of the Sailor, which teaches volunteer tour guides and reenactors about life in the Confederate navy. *Fort Jackson is three miles from Savannah off U.S. 80 (Island Expressway); 1 Fort Jackson Road, Savannah, GA 31404 (912) 232-3945.*

Fort Bartow

Built six hundred yards from Fort Jackson on Causton Bluff and intended to support it, this was the largest earthwork in the

Confederacy. Consisting of miles of heavy earthen walls, ditches, and magazines, it required two years to build. A marsh separated the inner works from an outer line that zigzagged along the river. A bombproof excavated here was one hundred feet by twenty feet and covered with ten feet of earth. Although the area is currently being developed for expensive homes, some of the fort may be preserved. *Fort Jackson is three miles from Savannah off U.S. 80 (Island Expressway); 1 Fort Jackson Road, Savannah, GA 31404 (912) 232-3945.*

Wormsloe

On Skidaway Narrows on the Isle of Hope, Wormsloe commands a back route to Savannah. During 1861–62 Confederates erected Fort Wimberly to protect this inland approach. The works were rarely garrisoned and never saw combat. The fort and a separate portion of earthworks may be seen on a walking tour. *Wormsloe State Historic Site, 7501 Skidaway Road, P.O. Box 13852, Savannah, GA 31406 (912) 352-2548; (912) 353-3023.*

Skidaway Island State Park

On the Sandpiper Nature Trail are earthworks that contributed to Savannah's defense. The square redoubt, with walls three to seven feet high and a ditch four to six feet deep, is the only infantry fort that survives of a chain that once surrounded Savannah and the outlying towns and plantations. *On Skidaway Island south of Savannah off Whitfield Avenue, 52 Diamond Causeway, Savannah, GA 31411 (912) 598-2300; (912) 598-2300.*

Fort Pulaski

Named for Polish patriot Casimir Pulaski who was killed fighting for Savannah during the American Revolution, this fort was constructed between 1829 and 1847. One of the engineers on the project was Robert E. Lee, who spent two years working on the dike and drainage system and returned thirty years later to inspect the Confederate defenses.

Five-sided Fort Pulaski faces the sea and is surrounded by a 7-foot-deep, 32- to 48-foot wide moat, which is crossed by a drawbridge. The structure is supported by wooden timbers driven 70 feet into the mud. The brick walls, 32 feet high and 11 feet thick, have a circumference of 1,580 feet and enclose a 2-acre parade ground. Inside the walls were officers quarters, ammunition magazines, and a variety of arched bombproofed chambers that housed cannon. Larger guns were positioned on top of the walls, but only 20 of 140 projected cannon were ever mounted. Large cisterns gathered two hundred thousand gallons of rain for a water supply. The fort, which cost one million dollars to build, contains twenty-five million bricks.

Fort Pulaski was considered the strongest brick fort in existence in January 1861 when Georgia Gov. Joseph Brown ordered it occupied before Union troops could arrive. Shortly after war broke out, one of the first priorities of the Federal army was to occupy Pulaski and deny the use of Savannah to blockade-runners. In November 1861 a Union force landed at Hilton Head and established a base. Working at night in absolute silence, the Federals hauled thirty-six cannon by hand over mud flats and placed them in eleven concealed batteries on nearby Tybee Island. Among the guns were newly developed rifled cannon.

On April 10, 1862, after the Confederate commander declined to surrender, the Union batteries began to bombard the fort, concentrating on the southeastern angle. The rifled shells burrowed into the wall before exploding, sending piles of brick into the moat and dismounting the Confederate guns. The bombardment continued throughout the night, and by the following day the angle had been demolished. Shells flying through the gap threatened to ignite the fort's magazine, which was directly opposite the breach and contained forty thousand pounds of powder. Faced with annihilation, the Confederates surrendered.

The Federals repaired the damaged walls in six weeks, mounted sixty guns, and maintained an eleven-hundred-man garrison in the fort until the end of the war. During 1864–65 part of the fort was used to house military and political prisoners. A cemetery where thirteen Confederates were buried has recently been found. The fort had a population of sixty cats to deal with rodents, but hungry prisoners caught and ate all but one. A picture of Union soldiers playing baseball here is the first photograph of that sport and probably the first time it was played in the South.

The brick walls of Fort Pulaski (above) crumbled under the April 1862 Union bombardment. During the Federal occupation, the fort's galleries (below) were crowded with Confederate prisoners.

The fort was abandoned in 1880, but the Federal government began restoring it in 1933 as a national park. Today it is an excellent example of a brick coastal fort. The visitors center houses a series of exhibits explaining how Pulaski was built and how it was conquered. Cannon have been remounted around the fort and rooms have been restored as quarters, mess rooms, and so forth to demonstrate daily garrison life. The magazines, cisterns, drawbridges, and other interesting features of the fort are visible. A walk around the fort shows the system of dikes and the damage that Fort Pulaski suffered. Many craters remain, and the demolished wall was repaired with a different color brick.

On the parapet is a bronze tablet honoring Lt. Christopher Hussey and Pvt. John Lathan, who re-raised the Confederate flag after it had been shot down during the bombardment.

A candlelight tour is featured annually, and twice a year reenactments are hosted. *Fort Pulaski National Monument is sixteen miles east of Savannah on U.S. 80; P.O. Box 30757, Tybee Island, GA 31410-0757 (912) 786-5787.*

In 1848 two lighthouses were constructed near Pulaski to guide ships upriver to Savannah. Both the Cockspur Island Light (South Channel Light) and its twin on Oyster Bed Island (North Channel Light) were darkened during the Civil War. Although Cockspur Island was directly in the line of fire between Confederate and Union artillery at Fort Pulaski, it was not damaged during the bombardment. To the left of the bridge over Lazeretto Creek, the eleven Union batteries were mounted along the shoreline. *East of U.S. 80 between Fort Pulaski and Tybee Island.*

Tybee Lighthouse and Museum

In a battery of old Fort Screven (Spanish-American War), the Tybee Museum offers a fascinating variety of exhibits describing coastal Georgia. In the Civil War Room are artifacts and displays relating to Fort Pulaski's bombardment, Sherman's March to the Sea, and the occupation of Savannah. *On Tybee Island opposite the lighthouse; turn onto Second Street off U.S. 80 and follow the signs; Tybee Museum and Lighthouse, 30 Meddin Drive, P.O. Box 366, Tybee Island, GA 31328 (912) 786-4077 (museum); (912) 786-5801 (lighthouse).*

While Union forces prepared to occupy Tybee Island as a base of operations against Fort Pulaski, retreating Confederates (the local Irish Jasper Greens) attempted to destroy the one-hundred-foot-tall brick lighthouse (1857) by igniting a keg of gunpowder at its base. A fire resulted that left the light useless until 1867. The Federals attempted to repair it, but the effort was abandoned when a foreman and four workers died of cholera. Confederates had also prepared defenses on Tybee, including a Martello tower that has since been demolished.

Rice Fields and Plantations

While Sherman and Hardee dueled on Savannah's perimeter, Confederate and Federal cavalry fought on Argyle Island for control of the Confederate escape route along the South Carolina shore. North of Savannah and Port Wentworth, U.S. 17 crosses the Houlihan Bridge to the island and then enters South Carolina through the Savannah National Wildlife Refuge. A brochure available at refuge headquarters guides visitors to rice plantations in the area where fighting occurred.

The Savannah Sugar Refining Company occupies the site of the Colerain Plantation, where concealed Union batteries opened on the CSS *Macon* and *Sampson,* which were attempting to escape upriver to Augusta. The ships collided, ran aground, and were captured. One of the sailors seized following the action was John Thomas Scharf, later the Confederacy's naval historian.

In this same area was Mulberry Plantation, where in 1793 Eli Whitney, a northern tutor, invented the cotton gin, which led to the expansion of slavery.

Near the Effingham County line is Monteith, where Gen. Henry W. Slocum established headquarters.

About three miles east of GA 307, where U.S. 80 crosses the railroad, is the spot where Sherman was exposed to Confederate artillery fire that decapitated a passing slave.

Sherman and the Seventeenth Corps approached Savannah along the Louisville Road (U.S. 80) through Pooler, where Sherman was angered by the placement of torpedoes in the road. This route was used by the withdrawing Confederates and the advancing Federals. Savannah's mayor met Union troops and officially offered the city's surrender to Gen. John W. Geary at the intersection of the Louisville Road with the Augusta Road (GA 21).

Dean Forrest Road (GA 307, between U.S. 80 and U.S. 17) parallels Sherman's lines, which were to the west. Union artillery batteries were erected at the sharp curve. The canals running alongside the road (and throughout Chatham County) were used to flood the marshes and rice fields that were studded with wicked timber barriers and separated the combatants. Confederate defenses paralleled the Union line to the east along Salt Creek. Piney Point Battery and Battery Jones were near the intersection of U.S. 17 and Dean Forrest.

U.S. 17 (Silk Hope Road) was the primary coastal route used during the Civil War. Southeast of U.S. 17-GA 204, Grove Point Road runs south toward Cheves Rice Mill, where Sherman watched the assault on Fort McAllister. The site is now private property. At Wild Herron Road along Grove Point Road is Wild Herron Plantation, a landmark of operations around Savannah. At the railroad on Chevis Road is the spot where Capt. William Duncan killed a mule on the tracks, forcing the last train out of Savannah to stop and be captured or be derailed.

U.S. 17 near the Bryan County line passes the sites of many Union camps and Lebanon Plantation, owned by Col. E. A. Anderson, commander of the Savannah River batteries.

The eighteen-mile-long Savannah and Ogeechee Canal, constructed to connect the two rivers in 1831, was renovated in 1848 with the addition of six brick locks, each 110 feet long. On December 6, 1864, Confederate forces fell back and used the barrier as part of Savannah's defense. Two locks are preserved at Savannah-Ogeechee Canal Park two miles west of I-95 and southwest of Pooler on Bush Road between GA 204 and Little Neck Road. Bush Road parallels the canal. A historical marker describes Civil War activity. The Federals advanced along the canal to the east toward Savannah.

GA 204 was the Fort Argyle–Old River Road along which the Fifteenth Corps advanced. They camped at the point where the canal enters the Ogeechee on December 8–9, where Duncan departed in his canoe for the coast (*see page 178*). Duncan drifted past Confederates at King's Bridge and brought the first notice to the Federal navy and the entire Union that Sherman had successfully marched across Georgia and had arrived at the Atlantic shore.

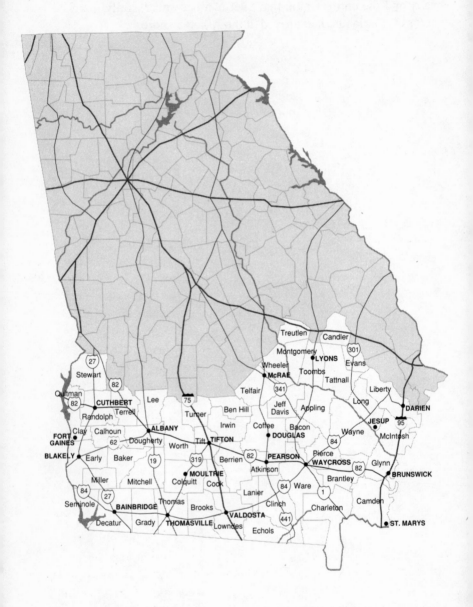

❧ 8 ❧

South Georgia

EXCEPT FOR ITS AREAS around the Atlantic Coast, south Georgia escaped the ravages of war, despite fears of a Federal amphibious assault from the Apalachicola River into the Chattahoochee and rumors of an overland attack from Florida. Because the coast was considered indefensible by Confederate officials, some towns were abandoned and their populations evacuated inland. The coastal islands were quickly occupied by Federal forces, and the great plantations in the region never recovered from their ruinous mistreatment during the occupation.

The area produced considerable foodstuffs and naval products for the Confederacy, and the people generously accepted the refugees from the fighting farther north, cared for wounded and sick Confederate soldiers, and even hosted Federal prisoners removed from Andersonville. Ironically, this peaceful area was the scene of the last act in the war—the capture of Jefferson Davis.

Fort Gaines

The Fort Gaines Female College was used to store food and wool, a one-tenth "tax in kind" levied by the Confederate government. The material was distributed to local families when the war ended. A wayside inn was maintained for soldiers here, and its records were kept on scraps of wallpaper.

In 1863 a fort with three cannon was established on the high bluffs overlooking the Chattahoochee River as protection against raids by Federal gunboats that might try to move on the industrial works at Columbus. The raids never occurred reportedly because the

Federals were unable to secure a reliable pilot. Late in 1864 some prisoners removed from Andersonville were transferred to the fort.

One artillery emplacement has been recreated with a cannon, and a second emplacement farther south is indicated by a depression on the river side of the road. Infantry trenches extended along the bluff. The third cannon was placed on the riverbank below, commanding a downstream bend. *In Frontier Village west of GA 39 on the river.*

New Park Cemetery. There are eighteen unidentified Confederate soldiers interred here. They died in local hospitals set up at the Male Seminary, which closed in 1862 when 103 students joined the Confederate army, and at the Fort Gaines Female College. The soldiers had been wounded at the battle of Olustee, Florida. The small memorial to the dead was placed in 1907. *In New Park Cemetery behind the nursing home at the intersection of GA 37 and GA 39.*

Lumpkin's Confederate guardian fills his pipe.

The houses used as wayside homes are marked on a tour map, which also notes the sites of the officers quarters, a depression where the magazine for the battery was stored, New Park Cemetery, and the recreated battery. The McAlister House (Jefferson Street between Troup and Hancock, 1850), used as the courthouse during the war, held a few Union prisoners.

Providence Chapel Christian Church (1837). Pastor Jubilee Smith left his pulpit to lead an infantry company made up of his parishioners. *On U.S. 280 three and one-half miles north of Richland.*

Lumpkin

On Old Chestnut Street, one block off Chestnut Street (U.S. 27) and west of the courthouse, is the home of Clement A. Evans, Confederate general in every Virginia campaign, prominent minister, and noted Southern historian of the war, having edited the twelve-volume *Confederate Military History* (1899). The stone Confederate soldier beside the historic courthouse is depicted casually filling his pipe. The memorial was dedicated on April 16, 1908.

Maimed by a tornado, a stone figure watches over Confederate graves in Cuthbert.

Cuthbert

Greenwood Cemetery. Twenty-four Confederates are buried here. They died between 1863 and 1865 in hospitals established at Andrew College (called the Hood Hospital, 413 College Street, where classes were suspended for three years) and the Baptist Female College (Hill Hospital). Also interred is Mary Joyner, "the Hospital Angel" who faithfully attended the wounded. A Confederate statue was erected here in 1896 on the downtown square, but a tornado toppled the stone soldier in 1909 and a new identical figure—a scout shading his eyes and peering into the distance—replaced it in 1910. The memorial is surrounded by four stone cannon. The original statue, missing a rifle, right arm, and left hand, watches over the

Confederates. *Greenwood Cemetery at the end of Oak and along Hamilton Street, south of U.S. 82.*

Blakely

The last original Confederate flagpole in Georgia, perhaps in the entire South, stands on the courthouse square. Cut by J. Wilke Brooks and Peter Pool from a long leaf pine, it was brought into town by a yoke of oxen and erected on May 16, 1861, by Thomas Williams and Isaac Layton. A ten-foot section of another timber was spliced onto the pole to make it one hundred feet high; it is eighteen inches in diameter. The pole was dedicated in front of the entire population with great ceremony, and the first flag was raised by Miss Sarah Powell. Most communities erected poles to fly the new flag after Georgia entered the Confederacy, but many were destroyed by Federal occupation forces during Reconstruction and others succumbed to decay or storms. It is said that this flagpole was ordered cut down by a Union officer, but three stalwart citizens—Luke Howard, B. Chancey, and Benjamin F. Fryer—threatened to kill the soldier who wielded the ax. After assurances that no Confederate flag would fly from the local landmark, the order was countermanded. The often-repaired pole today measures only sixty-five feet, and the American flag is flown above the Georgia flag. Also on the grounds is a Confederate monument, unveiled in 1909.

At nearby Safford the gunboat *Chattahoochee* was two years in building at the Confederate naval yard owned by David S. Johnston. Construction was supervised by Lt. Catesby ap R. Jones, who commanded the *Virginia* during her engagement with the *Monitor.*

Dawson

Gov. Joseph Brown arranged for three hundred refugees to be relocated here after Atlanta fell. Union troops occupied the "Exile Camp" until 1868. Sick and wounded soldiers were cared for at a wayside home by Dr. and Mrs. C. A. Cheatham. A potash mill, a gun shop, and other industries were relocated here when Federals occupied Rome and parts of northern Alabama.

Bainbridge

A cotton mill operated here by S. D. Tonge produced cloth for Confederate uniforms. In 1864 Tonge contributed twelve hundred mattresses for the care of Confederate wounded in Macon hospitals.

A statue of a Confederate soldier, carved in Italy from Carrara marble for three thousand dollars, was placed in Willis Park downtown, bordered by Water, Broad, West, and Broughton Streets. The monument, surrounded by two brass cannon, two large carronades, and a pool, was dedicated on April 26, 1905. Nearby is the Volunteers Monument, a plaque set on a stone, unveiled on April 24, 1936.

Greenwood Triangle (1919), at Tallahassee Highway and Lake Douglas Road, still has the drapes that were buried for safekeeping during the war.

Smithville

Federal cavalry searching for Jefferson Davis passed through in May 1865.

Albany

A hardtack factory operated by Col. Nelson Tift, the city founder, fed hungry Confederate soldiers. His packing house pickled pork, beef, and mutton for the navy. That facility was in the Bridge House, constructed by Tift in 1859 as a toll bridge across the Flint River. Tift Hall, above, was a residence, and the bridge passed through the center of the structure. Tift and his brother Asa built the ironclads *Mississippi* at New Orleans and *Atlanta* at Savannah. They operated a naval depot here to secure flour and cornmeal for the Confederacy. *112 North Front Street, now Keenan Auto Parts.*

Theatre Albany was constructed in the early 1860s by Capt. John A. Dawson, Confederate commissary officer for the southwest Georgia region, one of Georgia's breadbaskets. At the end of the war Dawson arranged the release of fifteen hundred bales of cotton seized by Union authorities. After the war he founded a lecture society that hosted Jefferson Davis and many Confederate generals. On display in the parlor is a chair used by Davis. Laura Keene, who was performing in *Our American Cousin* at Ford's Theatre when Lincoln was shot there, also performed the play here. *514 Pine Street, Albany, GA 31701 (912) 439-7141.*

A Confederate memorial, erected to honor the dead in 1901, is at the corner of Jackson and Pine. In Riverside Cemetery is a statue at the graves of seven unknown Confederates. A commemorative tablet was dedicated by the UDC in 1951.

Saint Teresa Catholic Church (315 Residence Avenue, 1859), on the National Register, was a Civil War hospital. A number of small corked morphine bottles found beneath the structure are displayed at the Thronateeska Heritage Museum.

Two houses on Broad Street and Washington Street served as wayside homes, providing passing soldiers with food, lodging, clothing, and transportation. Men trained in a camp established at Blue Springs, where ladies gathered to sew clothing and other articles for the soldiers. *Thronateeska Heritage Museum of History and Science, Heritage Plaza, 100 Roosevelt Avenue, Albany, GA 31707 (912) 432-6955.*

Pine Bloom was the Albany home of Alfred H. Colquitt, three-term governor, U.S. senator, and Confederate general. Iris Court was headquarters for Federal Gen. Joseph A. Cooper during the military occupation after the war.

Thomasville

This community had both hospitals and prisons during the war. In a sad counterpart to U. S. Grant's infamous "Jewish Order," in August 1862 Thomasville's Jewish community, blamed for economic troubles and accused of treason, was given ten days to evacuate. Sharp protests from the Jewish community in Savannah rebuked this and similar anti-Semitic newspaper campaigns in Macon and Savannah.

Laurel Hill Cemetery. Thirty-eight Confederate soldiers are buried here; their names are listed on a stone marker. Standing over the plot is a statue of Judgment, a woman in flowing robes. It was originally intended to grace the Savannah Confederate Monument but was rejected as unsuitable, and Thomasville acquired it. Confederate Gen. John C. Vaught (1824–75) is buried here. He was at First Manassas, surrendered at Vicksburg, and marched on Washington, D.C., with Jubal Early. As part of Jefferson Davis's cavalry escort in the flight from Richmond, Vaught was present at the final cabinet meeting in Washington, Georgia, where he was captured on May 9, 1865. *On Madison at Webster Street.*

Prisoner of War Camp. When Andersonville was threatened by Sherman's feint on the march to Savannah in November 1864, a seven-acre temporary prison was built here to hold five thousand prisoners who were transported on the Atlantic and Gulf Railroad from Blackshear. Part of the ditch that surrounded the prison, originally eight-feet deep and twelve-feet wide, remains in a park. The ditch was dug by slaves and guarded from the opposite embankment by guards and artillery, with fires burning at night to illuminate the makeshift facility. Prisoners were given axes to fell timber for shelter and fires, and falling trees killed two or three. Five hundred prisoners died from typhoid and smallpox at the First Methodist Church (425 North Broad Street; replaced in 1885) and the Fletcher Institute. Initially buried at the church, they were reinterred at Andersonville after the war. One Federal prisoner, E. W. Clark of Paris, Maine, died at nearby Greenwood Plantation and remains buried there. The prisoners marched sixty miles to Albany and boarded a train that returned them to Andersonville on Christmas Eve. *Wolfe Street.*

Thomas County Historical Society Museum. The museum displays three flags of local Confederate regiments and Confederate weapons, money, and bonds. *725 North Dawson Street, Thomasville, GA 31792 (912) 226-7664.*

On the courthouse square is an obelisk of Italian marble draped with the Confederate flag. It was dedicated in 1879. Greenville, one of Thomasville's many grand mansions, was supposedly the inspiration for Twelve Oaks in *Gone with the Wind.*

South of Thomasville, spanning the Ochlockonee River beside the new bridge on U.S. 91, is the Confederate Bridge, originally the Jones Bridge. Local authorities believe it was renamed as a memorial; if so, the records were lost.

Georgetown

A Federal cavalry brigade commanded by Gen. Benjamin H. Grierson, famed for a cavalry raid through Mississippi in 1863, camped nearby at war's end.

Sycamore

A five-foot square granite slab (1920s) honoring Turner County's Confederate soldiers is at the Turner Elementary School.

Ashburn

On Main Street South (GA 41) is a Jefferson Davis Highway marker.

Tifton

Tift County's Confederate monument is in Fulwood Park at the corner of Tift Avenue and Twelfth Street, dedicated on Confederate Memorial Day 1910. It has stood in five different locations.

Moultrie

The courthouse square contains a Confederate memorial, unveiled on April 26, 1911.

Quitman

West End Cemetery. The seventeen soldiers buried here died in area hospitals during the last year of the war. Memorial services have been conducted since 1869. Local tradition states that when a group of orphans from the Confederate home in Lauderdale, Mississippi, attended the services in 1871, one child discovered that her father was buried here. A stone monument has been erected in memory of the unknown dead. *West End Cemetery on West Screven Street at South Laurel Street.*

At the courthouse is a granite obelisk honoring Confederate dead, dedicated on April 26, 1879, and on Main Street is the statue of a Confederate soldier that was erected in 1921.

Fitzgerald

The story of this lovely city is actually post–Civil War. It began in the 1890s when successive droughts turned much of the Midwest into a dust bowl. At the same time, many aging veterans of the Union armies were seeking a place to live out their years removed from severe winters. In 1898 Philander H. Fitzgerald, an Indiana newspaper publisher and former drummer boy, was surveying the South for a potential "colony" for the patriots when Georgia Gov. William J. Northern, who had sent trainloads of food to the starving people of the drought area, offered one hundred thousand acres in southern Georgia. Fitzgerald accepted the kind offer, and within a year eight thousand men, women, and children had arrived from thirty-two states and two territories to hack out a flourishing community, complete with schools, churches, homes, shops, and even an opera house. Some had campaigned in Georgia with Sherman, a few had been imprisoned at Andersonville, and one was with the Union cavalry that had captured Jefferson Davis just a few miles south of here at Irwinville.

The Yankees were soon assimilated as many southerners moved into the new community, too. Streets were named for generals of both armies—Lee, Grant, Johnston, Sherman—and even the *Monitor* and the *Merrimack.* There was even a Lee-Grant Hotel, for many years the largest wooden structure in the state. The city celebrated both memorial days.

At Evergreen Cemetery are the graves of veterans from both armies. Also buried here is William Jordan Bush, the last of the 125,000 Georgians who served the Confederacy. Born in 1845, he was a private in Virginia under John B. Gordon. He died in Fitzgerald in 1952 at the age of 107.

Blue and Gray Museum. The community maintains this interesting museum in the former train depot. On display are numerous

Civil War artifacts, including flags, weapons, and uniforms donated by veterans of both sides, and photographs and murals that depict the history of a unique Georgia city. Also on exhibit are the mortar and pestle of Jefferson Davis's doctor and the huge mantel from the Lee-Grant Hotel. Fitzgerald is important as a symbol of how America began to unify just a few decades after the bitter war had ended. *Blue and Gray Museum, Municipal Building, P.O. Box 1285, Fitzgerald, GA 31750 (912) 423-5375.*

In the median of Jackson Street is a Jefferson Davis Highway marker.

Irwinville

On April 2, 1865, Robert E. Lee informed Jefferson Davis that Petersburg would have to be abandoned, which meant that Richmond was no longer defensible. Davis and his cabinet left the Confederate capital and spent a month traveling through North and South Carolina as the Confederacy slowly dissolved. On May 5 Davis dismissed the cabinet in Washington, Georgia, and passed through Sandersville, Dublin, and Abbeville trying to make his way to Texas, where considerable Confederate troops remained that Davis hoped would carry on the struggle. Meanwhile, Lee surrendered at Appomattox and Lincoln was assassinated. The new president, Andrew Johnson, implicated Davis in the assassination plot and offered a reward of one hundred thousand dollars for his capture. Davis, his family, and a small escort camped on the night of May 9 near the village of Irwinville.

The previous day two separate units of Federal cavalry, part of the massive manhunt for Davis, had stumbled upon the trail. At dawn they rushed the camp. The surprised Confederates offered no resistance, but in the early morning darkness a spirited skirmish broke out between the two Union commands, each believing the other to be Davis's guard. Two Northern soldiers died before the tragic mistake was realized. They were the last casualties of the Civil War.

Davis was captured and immediately sent to Macon, where he traveled by train to Augusta, and from there by ship to Fort Monroe, Virginia. He was imprisoned for two years on charges of treason.

James A. Clements, a local witness to Davis's capture, intended that the site of the president's capture should be a Southern shrine. His son and others donated the land to the state for a park. A Confederate museum displays Civil War relics, including part of a tree that stood where Davis was seized. On the grounds is a memorial topped by a bronze bust of the Confederate president, dedicated in 1936, marking the exact spot of his capture. The twelve-acre park was run by the state of Georgia until 1977 and is now maintained by volunteers and the Irwin County Commission. *Jefferson Davis Memorial Park is two miles north of Irwinville, off GA 32; Route 2, Box 289-B, Fitzgerald, GA 31760 (912) 831-2335.*

At the crossroads in Irwinville is a Jefferson Davis Highway marker.

Ocilia

A Confederate monument, erected in 1911, is on the courthouse lawn.

Douglas

Across from the railroad station is a Confederate monument, unveiled October 10, 1911.

Valdosta

The statue of a Confederate soldier overlooking the courthouse grounds was dedicated on October 20, 1911. The Lowndes County Historical Society and Museum, in the Carnegie Library (1913), has exhibits concerning the area's participation in the Civil War and two important war-related industries: naval stores and sea-island cotton. *305 West Central Avenue, P.O. Box 434 (31603-0434) Valdosta, GA 31601 (912) 247-4780.*

Blackshear

A temporary prison camp was established here in November 1864 for five thousand Union captives from Magnolia Springs. It was closed in January 1865. *Off GA 203 north of Blackshear.*

Waycross

Ware County's Confederate veterans are honored by a monument erected in Phoenix Park beside the courthouse in 1910. In front of the statue is a cannon that prevented Sherman's troops from crossing the Altamaha River and burning the vital Gulf Railroad bridge near Doctortown in December 1864. It was spiked and abandoned until 1887, when railroad officials transported it to Waycross. Jefferson Davis spoke on May 3, 1886, to the assembled populace while passing through on a train.

Wayne County

Doctortown. The railroad bridge protected by the cannon now in Waycross is found east of U.S. 84 on the dirt Doctortown Landing Road, past several huge timber plants. North of the river is Long County, which foraging Union cavalry terrorized during Sherman's siege.

Appling County

Confederate recruits trained near Graham.

Liberty County

While consolidating the siege lines around Savannah, Sherman sent his cavalry south to destroy the Savannah and Gulf Railroad and to forage for provisions. Judson Kilpatrick established his headquarters at historic Midway Church and burned a church in Sunbury to signal its capture to Sherman and the Union navy in Ossabaw Sound.

Midway Church (1792)

The beautiful church, a museum in a recreated eighteenth-century home next door, and the notable graveyard (established 1754) across the highway are open to visitors. The communion table in the church was used as a meat block by Northern cavalry, who badly damaged the magnificent structure while camped here for two weeks and foraging in the area, which they stripped of livestock and other provisions. The original wooden gate to the graveyard was burned by the Federals, who used the cemetery as an animal pen. At Riceboro they also tore a beautiful metal gate (1853) off the parade ground of the Liberty Independent Troop. Surviving members mounted it here in 1867. *On U.S. 17 in Midway. Midway Museum, P.O. Box 195, Midway, GA 31320 (912) 884-5837.*

Sunbury

The town was never rebuilt after the war, but a state historic site preserves an earthen fort from the War of 1812, which was used by Confederate sentries. A museum explains the history of Sunbury, and a mural depicts Sunbury's destruction by Federal cavalry. *Eight miles east of I-95; follow the signs; Fort Morris State Historic Site, Route 1, P.O. Box 236, Midway, GA 31320 (912) 884-5999.*

Hinesville

A cavalry skirmish occurred here on December 16, 1864. Liberty County contributed many horse soldiers to the Confederacy, and their monument, dedicated at the courthouse on January 19, 1928, features a rare cavalryman, although a rather diminutive one.

Fort Stewart Museum

Although this museum concentrates on the history of the Twenty-fourth Infantry Division and Fort Stewart since its inception in 1941, it does display a few Civil War artifacts. Some of the units now composing the Twenty-fourth fought in the Civil War for the Union, but a Georgia National Guard contingent based here traces its history to the Confederate military. *Corner of Wilson and Utility Streets, Fort Stewart, Hinesville, GA 31313 (912) 767-7885.*

McIntosh County

On Butler Island, to the south on U.S. 17, is a seventy-five-foot-high chimney from a steam-powered rice mill. It marks the plantation of Pierce Butler, who married British actress Fanny Kemble in 1834. Their two-month stay on the island led to arguments over the morality of slavery and their divorce. Alarmed upon hearing support for the Confederacy and slavery in the North and in England, in 1863

Fanny published her *Journal of a Residency on a Georgia Plantation, 1838–1839,* which was a powerful indictment of slavery.

In November 1862 raiders from a Union gunboat in the Sapleo
River stripped Marlow Plantation on the bluff overlooking Pine
Harbor. During other Federal raids most of a Confederate cavalry
company and a defense force consisting of twenty-three elderly
men were captured. Alerted by spies that the aged defenders would
be meeting on August 3, 1864, at Ebenezer Church, nine miles
north of Darien, the Federals captured the party, then marched
them to Darien, where they were shipped to a Northern prison.
That action left only Company F, Third South Carolina Cavalry,
under Lt. W. L. Male, to patrol the coast and guard against Union
raids. On August 18 Federals landed by ship and surprised the
Confederates so thoroughly that only twenty escaped. Five civilians were seized and the South Newport River bridge, at U.S. 17,
was burned.

Darien

Because the town could not be defended, Confederates evacuated
Darien. In June 1863 black Union troops, the Fifty-fourth Massa-
chusetts under Col. Robert Gould Shaw, came from Saint Simon's
Island to burn the town. Tabby foundations from the destroyed
buildings are found along the river below the visitors center on U.S.
17. The Methodist church on Vernon Square, partially destroyed in
1863, was rebuilt in 1884 using much of the original material.
Nearby is Laurel Grove Plantation, the birthplace of John McIntosh
Kell (1823–1900), executive officer of the renowned sea raiders
Sumter and *Alabama* and later adjutant general of the state of Georgia. Also nearby is the site of Jonesboro, where women, children,
and convalescents took refuge from Union raids.

Sapelo Island

Sapelo Island Light on the Altamaha River served the port of Darien.
Constructed in 1820, it is sixty-five feet high and twenty-eight feet
at the base. Confederates removed the lens and dismantled other
important machinery when they evacuated the area in March 1862.
The light was not repaired until 1868. Most slaves had been removed
to Baldwin County when Federals vandalized Thomas Spalding's

mansion, South End House. Union ships stopped here during the war to raid for supplies. Sapelo Island can only be reached by ferry, and tickets are sold at the Darien Welcome Center. *Sapelo Island National Estuarine Research Reserve, P.O. Box 15, Sapelo Island, GA 31327 (912) 485-2251.*

Glynn County

Saint Simon's Island

The island and most coastal positions were abandoned as indefensible in early 1862 on the advice of Robert E. Lee. In February a Union officer noted "fortifications of great strength" constructed on Saint Simon's by Confederates, and fires dotted the horizon for three days as Georgians torched property. The works consisted of heavy palmetto logs covered with twenty feet of dirt. One fort had a roof of railroad iron laid on massive wooden beams and covered with ten feet of earth. Fort Brown stood beside the lighthouse, which was destroyed by retreating Southerners to prevent its use as a navigational marker. A new one-hundred-foot-high lighthouse was erected on the site in 1872. On the second floor of the lighthouse keeper's cottage next door are displays of local history, including Civil War memorabilia and a video history of the light. A chain marker indicates the site of the seventy-five-foot-tall Civil War lighthouse (1810). *The Museum of Coastal History, at the intersection of King's Way, Ocean Boulevard, and Demere Road, 101 Twelfth Street, Saint Simon's Island, GA 31522 (912) 638-4666.*

One of the most beautiful spots in Georgia is Christ Episcopal Church on Frederica Road near Fort Frederica. The structure (1828; rebuilt 1886) was substantially damaged by Union soldiers who took target practice at the church, smashed the organ, broke windows, burned pews, and used the altar as a butcher's block. In the scenic cemetery is the grave of Henry Lord Page King, a young Confederate whose body was returned from Fredericksburg, Virginia, by a servant.

Rich local resident Thomas Butler King was a special commissioner of the Confederacy to England. Tabby ruins remaining from his impressive estate, Retreat Plantation, are incorporated in the Sea Island Golf Club.

burned pews, and used the altar as a butcher's block. In the scenic cemetery is the grave of Henry Lord Page King, a young Confederate whose body was returned from Fredericksburg, Virginia, by a servant.

Rich local resident Thomas Butler King was a special commissioner of the Confederacy to England. Tabby ruins remaining from his impressive estate, Retreat Plantation, are incorporated in the Sea Island Golf Club.

Jekyll Island

When the Civil War broke out, one of the first Federal objectives was to seize the coastal islands to use as staging bases for blockading Southern ports. With this in mind, the Confederates built a five-gun battery that mounted one large 42-pounder and four 32-pounder naval cannon to protect Jekyll. When the island was evacuated, the population was moved inland for protection and Robert E. Lee obtained Governor Brown's permission to remove the guns for use in Savannah's defenses. In March 1862 Federal troops occupied the island. The battery is visible on the west side of Jekyll, opposite a historical marker and across the airstrip.

On display at the wharf on Riverview Drive is the mess kettle of the slave yacht *Wanderer,* which was the last vessel to transport slaves from Africa to the United States, landing on Jekyll in 1858. The ship was captured by Federal authorities in 1861 and saw duty as a gunboat around Pensacola.

Saint Marys Methodist Church was used as a Union quartermaster storehouse.

Brunswick

A Union diary recorded that this city was found abandoned, "as is the case with the entire coast." Plantations were inhabited by the oldest and youngest slaves, the fit having been taken with the refugees. Occupation forces lived well off the abandoned crops. A Confederate monument honoring Glynn County's Confederate veterans stands in Hanover Park at the end at Newcastle.

Camden County

Saint Marys

Waterfront buildings were destroyed by Union gunboat shelling, although the residential area survived, and many residents fled to the interior. When Federal forces occupied the city in 1862, they closed the Saint Marys Methodist Church (1858) on Conyers Street until 1865 and used it as a quartermaster store, butchering cattle and sheep there. The Episcopal church on Wheeler Street was built to replace the one destroyed by the Federals.

On GA 40 Spur between Saint Marys and Crooked River, opposite Kings Bay Naval Base, are the extensive and well-preserved remains of a tabby building (1825) that produced starch during the Civil War. *Crooked River State Park, 3092 Spur 40, Saint Marys, GA 31558 (912) 882-6200.*

These tabby ruins on the coast housed a factory that produced starch during the war.

son sent a tombstone in 1833 and probably visited the grave while he was stationed at Fort Pulaski in 1830 and again in January 1862 on his inspection tour of Confederate coastal defenses. The island was occupied by Federals after the white residents fled. In 1870 Lee returned, finding Dungeness "burned and the island devastated." His daughter, Agnes, decorated her grandfather's grave with flowers. In 1912 the Virginia legislature reinterred Lee beside his son in the crypt at Washington and Lee University in Lexington. The original gravestone remains, with a slab explaining the removal of Lee's remains.

Andrew Carnegie's brother, Thomas, erected an enormous, two-hundred-room mansion that poachers burned in the 1950s. Its huge ruins remain.

A forty-five-minute ferry ride, operated by the National Park Service, is required to reach the island, where the ruins of Dungeness remain just south of the ferry landing. A trail leads to the cemetery. The ferry runs twice a day to this popular wilderness area, and it is wise to call ahead to reserve space since only three hundred visitors a day are allowed. *Cumberland Island National Seashore, P.O. Box 806, Saint Marys, GA 31558 (912) 882-4336.*

⇜ Indexes ⇝

Confederate Prisons

Forts and Earthworks

Confederates

Federals

Museums and Homes